i

I Must Be in Heaven, a promise kept

Copyright © 2007 by Valerie Anne Faulkner

ISBN 978-0-615-19951-1

First Edition 2008

This is a true story, some names have been changed as per request.

Printed in the United States of America

F.E.I. Publishing

Cover Art by Shaye N. Ayre

I Must Be in Heaven, a promise kept

Valerie Anne Faulkner

www.imustbeinheaven.com

Acknowledgements

To our Family and friends who supported us in our time of need.

Shaye Ayre: For her fine artistry in designing the cover.

William C. Faulkner III (Billy): For taking over the job as head of the family.

Stacie Selover: For keeping our heads on straight when we bugged her for grammar corrections.

Our Grandchildren: Katie, Maggie, Abbie, Kyle, and Lily.

Sandy Laniewicz: For editing and proof reading.

To the Doctors and staff at Morton Plant Hospital who worked so professionally and diligently.

To John Ritter and Prayer Warriors' everywhere.

To all the Angels who played a part in this story.

And willingly and proudly to our Heavenly Father

We thank you.

Valerie and Bill Faulkner

Dedication

It really wasn't that long ago; I remember it so well. Sweetly he sang to me along with the folk singer Glen Yarborough. "Come Share My life, you can make it wonderful." I listened to the lyrics that winter evening in 1967 and fell in love with the song and Bill. He wanted me, he needed me, and Bill told me, I'd be his wife.

Wife? Share his life? Have his children? Grow old together? At seventeen I was too young to envision but eager to dream. So, I smiled and sang along, "Come share my life, you too can make it wonderful, oh so beautiful, for two hearts so much in love."

Surely, it really doesn't seem that long ago; I remember it so well. I wanted him, I needed him, and I told him yes...... I'd share his life.

Today, I would like to invite you to come share our life. You'll understand why I have dedicated my first novel to: My husband, my best friend, William C. Faulkner Jr.

Prologue

"Oh, shit!" Startled by the sound of his voice, I awoke and mentally shook my head to clear the sleep from my brain. I suddenly understood the meaning of Bill's words.

"Are you late?"

"No... well, maybe just a little. I didn't hear the alarm and have to hurry. It's seven o'clock." He stretched and stood up.

Through sleepy eyes, I could see his naked body. I loved looking at Bill. Even after so many years, a thrill quivered inside me. I didn't want to move as I watched him pull up his jeans. His bare bottom quickly disappeared into the blue denim, and I heard him close the zipper.

Savoring my mind's thoughts while slipping out from under the covers, my feet found the floor. I reached for my comfy old house dress. Mm, the smell of clean cotton dried in fresh air was so pleasant. I sensed Bill's gaze as the dress slid down over my naked skin. I had this dress for so many years. With its scoop neck, cap sleeves, and buttons down the front it has only gotten better with age. Years ago, I had asked Mom to sew the buttons closed permanently. I just needed to pull the dress over my head.

Bill came closer and playfully gave me a hug, leaning down he kissed my neck. "Mm... Don't get me started... you did want breakfast, didn't you?" I ventured down the hallway, and quickly combed my fingers through my hair. Piling it at the top of my head, I secured a hair band in place. As I descended the oak wood treads, the only sound heard in the quiet of the morning was our dog Jake's claws tapping on the hard surface as he followed me.

Entering the kitchen, I flipped on the light and was glad I hadn't left any dirty dishes in the sink from the night before. The white countertop tiles looked so clean, and our new stainless steel appliances were stunning. They'd replaced old ivory ones and the new look still amazed me.

While I started to make the coffee, Jake seemed bewildered to see me moving around so early. He's such a smart dog. We got him as a puppy. Turning nine this year, he is beginning to show his age. He hadn't raced me down the stairs but instead followed me rather cautiously. This morning he didn't take his usual place in the middle of the kitchen floor where I would have to step over him but instead sat next to me looking up with quizzical eyes. His face showed so much expression. I looked at him and said, "Daddy's got school today. Okay?" For a moment, he paused then seeming to accept this explanation, left me for his favorite spot.

Since last year we've made it a point not to get up before eight. It's our way of giving ourselves benefits as members of the self-employed. We indulge ourselves until the sun shining through our bedroom window wakes us up. It's been nice; just a small treat. Today, however, Bill had to get up earlier. He was required to attend a continuing education class that began at eight o'clock. He needed the fourteen credits to renew his electrical contractor's license. I promised I'd rise with him and make breakfast. While I let water run into the pot, I placed a bagel in the toaster and found the cream cheese. It was usually closer to eleven o'clock by the time we ate. This was really too early for food – and definitely too early for multi-tasking.

"Coffee, I need coffee!" Bill yawned as he came down the stairs. I handed him a hot cup of fresh brew and asked if he actually wanted that bagel in the toaster. "Nah. Coffee will be fine. I need to wake up."

He'd shaved and washed his face and was dressed. He looked so handsome and appeared alert and ready to go. I reminded him to take his pill and asked,

"Do you need paper and pen?"

"No – well, yes – I mean, I took my pill. I don't need paper. Books and all are supplied or should be for two hundred bucks!"

We still had a few minutes until Bill had to leave. Jake needed to go outside so we opened the sliding glass door to the porch and followed, pulling up chairs at the glass-topped patio table. Bill commented, "I wish I hadn't slept through the alarm." Shrugging his shoulder he smiled and gave me a little wink. "Thank you for the second cup of coffee. I think it's starting to work."

I watched as the sun started to peek through the trees. How beautiful that bright orange ball looked. It certainly meant another hot day ahead of us. I was glad I didn't actually have to go out to work. I would stay home and clean house and get caught up on the office tasks. Laundry needed to be done, too, and, oh yes, deposits to the bank and groceries. I'd better make a list. I wished the coffee would start working on me. I really felt like a robot not truly awake, just in motion.

"Well Honey-Bunch, I gotta go." As he stood up, he placed the cell phone in his pocket. "I'll call you at break time."

"Okay – drive carefully. Be safe. I love you," I told him as he headed to the front door. When he got to the door he turned around, knowing I'd be right behind him. He gave me a great big hug, almost picking me up, and then a kiss. He felt so good, "I don't want to let you go."

"Gotta go... I'll be back before you know it..." Giving me a pat on my bottom and one more kiss, he left to get into his van. I stood at the screen door so that when he pulled out of the driveway he'd see me waving. As he looked back he held his hand in a single wave and beeped the horn quickly three times.

"I love you, too!"

I returned to the porch with another cup of coffee. The gray painted wood planks creaked as I walked over to my favorite wicker chair. Sitting down, I brought my knees up to get my bare feet off of the cool deck flooring. Curled up, I sat in awe of the beautiful morning that God had given me. Serene and quiet, nature had yet to fully awaken. The sky was cloudless except for a few hues of pink streaking just above the horizon. I thought about Bill driving and wondered if the morning sun was impairing his vision. After so many months this was the first time Bill was venturing out alone, and I knew today was a huge stepping stone for the both of us, yet I couldn't seem to release the fears that continually rushed into my thoughts. I wondered if I should call him to make sure he was safe. "No!" I said out loud. "I've got more faith than that! Lord, I know you'll watch over my love, my hero, my husband. Let me rejoice and remember the miracles. Give me the words to tell others that they may know how merciful and good you are."

Continuing to stare out into our backyard, I had tears welling in my eyes. I could smell the scent of gardenias and wished my heart could remember how it felt to be carefree. Wiping my eyes with the hem of my dress, I glanced over to the stoop and could see the blossoms that covered the bush just outside our screen room. Ever so gently they waved in the breeze. My thought's drifted and I wondered...*maybe this was God's plan for me. Could this quiet time be exactly what I needed?*

***

At the fireplace

I'd been keeping a journal for quite some time. A month had past and I'd not even looked at my notes. I walked back into the kitchen. Just where I'd left them, the pages were stretched out along the fireplace hearth in disorder. The files containing my notes, bits and pieces of white notebook paper, were strewn about. Just a few had been typed and stapled together. I wished I could wave a magic wand with sparkly sprinkle dust and make them all start shuffling about until one neat, organized manuscript appeared. I knew I needed to get all my deepest thoughts: the paragraphs of fulfillment, the sequences of happiness, true love and dismay – all into some kind of logical order. There was a story to be told about a girl (me) and a boy (Bill). The story was somewhere in this pile. I knelt down on the tile floor to get a closer look. Seeing the ragged-edged pages and post-it notes scribbled with hasty scrawls, whatever had been previously attempted was no longer clear to me. Was this the best I could do?

I thumbed through the pages. A sentence popped out at me as though highlighted. I read aloud, '*The sirens could be heard coming down the street until they ended in an abrupt death...silence.*' Seeing my handwriting, I wondered how I could relive that day in black and white. But I'd made a promise over a year ago.

Chapter 1

It was Monday, May 9th, and a beautiful spring morning. Bill and I had spent most of our weekend cleaning house and fine-tuning any discrepancies in preparation for our latest project: selling our home. The house was immaculate and we felt ready for the challenge.

Bill and I had new dreams and plans. We had placed our house on the market the previous week, and the realtor had said this day, after advertising, would probably be the day for customers to want to take a look. We'd known that ads were placed in the real estate magazines over the weekend and figured we'd better make sure everything was perfectly tidy for any lookers. So, beds were made and everything sparkled and smelled just wonderful.

We sat with our coffee and stared at perfection. We giggled with optimism about how the first person to see our home would probably say, "This is it! I must have this wonderful house! I will gladly pay any amount of money. I will pay even more than the asking price as long as I can have it!" We laughed and then stopped to gulp, because this was our home. There was a fine line between excited and utterly horrified that someone would actually want it. Finally, we just held hands and sat quietly, knowing that what will be, will be.

We enjoyed the moment and decided we had better get ready for work. We usually left home about 10:30 and this day would be no different. I dressed and was waiting for Bill to come downstairs. He usually went up to the bathroom and would finish getting dressed after I was done, and then the two of us would go do electrical work together. He held all the licenses and was lead man, but I always felt I gave him exceptional help – and the two of us made a great team! I took care of most of the paperwork and scheduling and assisted him on the job. We did very well and kept active throughout the day going on one service call to the next. He had taught me how to do wiring and many of our customers enjoyed watching the two of us accomplish our tasks. We worked in harmony and rarely had any conflicts. This amazed practically everyone we met. Being best friends, our work was merely an extension of play for the both of us.

Heat was the only debilitating problem that could become a threat to our livelihood. Bill was starting to have some concern with the hot summer days that were surely going to arrive too soon. Temperatures seemed to elevate earlier each year. Occasionally having to go into attics made his job treacherous. I assured him that after the 15th of the month he could excuse himself from attic work and we would pass those jobs on to our son's business. Of course, if the house sold, we could semi-retire. What a heavenly thought.

Just before 11:00 I heard a call from upstairs – or should I say a yell – from Bill. "VAL!" I couldn't imagine what his emergency was but yelled back, "Coming!" and went up to see. As I ran up the steps, I imagined Jake had left a package or worse yet the toilet was overflowing.

I certainly never expected to see Bill holding his head, then neck, then his legs, all in agonizing pain. I couldn't believe my eyes as he lay across our bed. I knew whatever was happening wasn't good.

"I'm calling 911." I felt my heart beating faster and my limbs feeling shaky, as I didn't know what was happening to him. When the operator answered, I told her we needed help. She calmly replied that she would send help but needed to ask me some questions and could I answer them? "Yes," I said. I had used the phone upstairs in the hallway, but it had a cord. I franticly explained, "I need to get the cordless phone." I can't even remember going downstairs, but I grabbed the cordless phone, unlocked the front door, and ran back up. I breathlessly told her, "I'm ready." Her calm voice assured me help was already on the way. She sounded like an angel. Bill was not looking very good. As we spoke, I got a wet cloth to cool Bill's brow. He was sweating profusely. The blanket he laid upon was already drenched. Time seemed to move in slow motion. I held onto the phone as though it were my only life line and listened to the operator's calming voice. I could feel my body trembling as I gave her the information. One more time she promised me: "Help will be arriving very soon." The sirens could be heard coming down the street until they ended in an abrupt death...silence. Red reflections throbbing on the front windows of our bedroom revealed the ambulance accompanied by a fire truck, here at our home. Oh, God, for my husband!

I put Jake in the bathroom knowing he could get so excited greeting new visitors. I told the operator, "They're here." Then I thanked the lady on the phone and pushed the end button. I stood at the foot of the bed as though paralyzed. I heard people entering my house. I shouted, "Up here!" and heard the pounding on each step as the EMTs bounded up the stairwell. A woman and two men entered our master bedroom. They quickly moved towards Bill as I moved to the side of the bed by his dangling feet so they could work. They didn't attempt to move him, just started with immediate actions of emergency care. None of us spoke. As though rehearsed, we just moved about without cues. I watched in silence and hoped their expertise would be enough. They had a large black bag filled with emergency equipment, and while one was taping wires to Bill, another was getting a hypodermic needle ready. I felt as though I was watching a movie, completely disconnected from what I was observing. I remember screaming for Jesus to help me and Bill. I was powerless and couldn't seem to believe what was happening. I said over and over, "Jesus,

Jesus, Jesus!" The EMTs continued to do their job as I prayed out loud, "Jesus, Jesus – please take care of my Bill!" In my distorted bubble I hovered, desperately attempting to comprehend what was happening. Terror had its strong grip on me; my fear was overwhelmingly intense.

With concern, yet sternness, the female EMT told me to move away from Bill's feet, as I might get kicked. These were the first words that had been spoken, quickly bursting my bubble. I suddenly understood. Bill was going through a violent seizure. He shook all over and foam bubbled from his mouth. I stared at him in disbelief. I couldn't face this. Frightened, I closed my eyes and yelled again for Jesus. They administered hoses and did things I didn't understand. One of the men asked me, "How much does Bill weigh?" They wanted to place him on a chair for the downstairs delivery. I responded, "About 210 pounds." Moments later another man, who was called by walkie-talkie, came into our room. They placed Bill on a chair – he couldn't be on a gurney at this point because patients can slide off when coming down the stairs. Strapped around his chest and across his lap, he was slumped and lifeless. Oh, God, I wondered, was he dead? I was terrified as they moved him carefully. I hung back in the hallway. I couldn't watch them retreat down the stairs. I stopped and prayed, "Please, Lord, let them all get downstairs safely." They did. I joined them at the bottom of the steps. Bill was placed on a rolling bed and then strapped on. The EMTs moved the stretcher out the door and down the walk to the driveway then safely put Bill in the back of the ambulance. They said I could ride with them.

"I'd like to ride in the back with Bill."

The driver said, "No, up front."

I said, "No, with Bill!"

Unrelenting, he said, "No, up front!"

"Okay," I sighed and entered the passenger side of the

ambulance. I noticed neighbors gathering around as they watched and wondered what had happened. The EMTs told me that it may have been a stroke which I relayed to the neighbors. My next door neighbor, Ann Marie, could see how frightened I was.

She said, "I'll follow you, but first I'll lock up the house and check on Jake." She waved as we headed out, sirens blaring, at a fast yet safe pace for the neighborhood. When we reached the highway, the ambulance accelerated, cutting through traffic like a knife through butter.

I called my sister Joyce from my cell phone and told her what I was doing. She said, "I'll meet you at the hospital." I was numb and too scared to be scared. Life felt blurry and weird. My brain was confused and my heart was agonizing. Could this be happening? Was this a delusion, a morbid prank that I was caught in and couldn't be set free of? I again felt life moving in slow, slow motion. I was seeing everything clearly yet, as distinct as it was, it wasn't clear enough to comprehend. It seemed like I was disconnected from reality and stuck in some strange, unnatural parallel existence.

Having flown down the streets, we came to a safe landing halting just before the emergency room entrance. I was immediately corralled into a reception area and bombarded with questions. I just wanted to be with Bill. He was wheeled to a part of the ER where desperate measures were being taken to keep him alive. I answered questions like address, phone number, his full name and birthday, his social security number (which I actually knew and remembered), and on and on. I just kept asking, "When can I see him?" My sister and Ann Marie arrived and tried to keep me calm. Joyce, being a nurse, did not have her usual 'it's okay' look on her face but instead showed major concern. More than I wanted to see. She wanted to speak with someone in authority so we might find out what was happening inside the E.R.

I needed to call the children, our grown children. Stacie,

our oldest, a middle-school teacher came immediately. Her husband and one of our granddaughters, Katie, also arrived; then Shaye, our youngest, shortly afterwards. Billy, who was about a half hour away, left his crew to work and arrived in a surprisingly short time. Once the kids were all there, I noticed how frightened they seemed; this was something awful, and this was happening to their Dad. This was happening to all of us. I kept thinking that if they would just let me see Bill I would feel better. I could help soothe away our children's fears. I finally insisted, "I must see him!" This request worked. However, the nurse informed us, "Not for too long. He's being red lighted to Morton Plant Hospital in Clearwater." She wasn't telling us what happened, just that it was serious. The kids followed in behind me, one at a time touching him, telling him to hang in there, telling Bill they loved him. I knew it was the words they wanted to remember saying, just in case. I told Bill, too, that I loved him and that I would meet him at Morton Plant Hospital. He was incoherent. He thrashed about and struggled as if fighting off some wild creature. His arms and body had been tied to the bed. The ER nurses and doctors had inserted IV's and placed tubes in his nose prohibiting Bill from speaking, even if he could. I finally was told to leave as they were getting him ready for his journey. I held his hand and prayed to our Lord, "Please watch over Bill." I told him one more time, "I love you, honey. I love you so much." He instinctively squeezed my hand four times.

Chapter 2

I let my hand slip from Bill's very loose grip. Just our finger-tips touched. Hesitating for a moment, I turned away holding the tips of my own fingers, wishing I could save the feeling forever. As I approached the door, Billy reached out to give me his hand and walked me out to the parking lot. I wondered why I hadn't yet realized that he had become a man, so much like his dad. Billy was tall and handsome, and holding onto his rough, working man's hand, I felt the pride that only a mother can feel. He had stepped up to the plate and revealed a sense of security that only the head of a family can extend.

Bill left immediately, red lighted (an ambulance term) to Morton Plant Hospital. I needed to get some clothes. The kids drove me back to the house so I could pack a few items and then we all discussed the route we would take to Clearwater. Stacie suggested we should take two cars. She was willing to drive the Jeep. Shaye said, "That will be fine. I'll drive my car and take Billy with me." They seemed to have it all worked out, and I couldn't even pretend to give a hoot; I just wanted to get going.

Stacie got behind the wheel and rearranged all the mir-rors. She pushed the seat way back to accommodate her long legs, and we both put on our seat belts. She started the engine and tried to find reverse. It had been along time since she had driven a standard transmission. Backing out the driveway, Stacie stalled the Jeep three times and swore at least twice, but it's kind of like riding a bike and in no time at all we were driving down the boulevard and merging onto U.S. Highway

19.

The trek takes about an hour and twenty minutes, and I must admit I zoned out for most of the ride. The adrenalin that had rushed through my body was wreaking havoc; tremors of fright rattled inside of me. I was already feeling the aftershock which was draining me. Terrified, my body just kept quivering. Involuntary movements were keeping me aware of the situation at hand yet, remarkably, no tears came. With my fists clenched, arms crossed over my chest, I attempted to try and control the shaking. I inwardly pleaded with God, "Please, please watch over my beloved husband."

Stacie concentrated on the highway traffic, occasionally asking, "Mom, are you doing okay?" She was aware of the shaking rippling the whole length of my body.

"I'm trying, honey. Don't worry about me. Watch the road. Thank you for driving. I love you."

"Love you too, Mom."

I've heard when one feels so desperate life can flash before you like a movie. My mind's eye brought a reprieve when I replayed the memories of the way Bill and I met.

***

It was July of 1962 when my grandparents invited my sister Joyce and me to Florida for summer vacation. They were driving down from New York, and my Mom thought she'd take a short break from work and travel with us too, to help with the driving. The five of us departed for the sunshine state.

It was definitely going to be a long drive. Back then, the interstate highway system was still only a dream. Highway 301 was the only way south, and it was just two lanes most of the way. Mom screaming at Grandpa is one part of the trip that really stands out in my memory; we got stuck behind a very slow traveling tractor, and Grandpa decided to pass on the solid yellow line. I didn't drive then – I just rode – and I will never forget that close call with an oncoming eighteen-wheeler. I probably wouldn't have known what was going on except for poor Mom. She about stood up in her seat as we swerved back to our lane, just in time, ahead of the old man on his tractor. After the initial fright, her tearful scolding definitely got Grandpa's attention. She must have made an impression; for the rest of the trip he could have been nominated for a safe driver award.

We helped the hours pass by singing songs. Over and over, Joyce and I sang our favorites: One Hundred Bottles of Beer on the Wall, The Song That Never Ends and my Grandmother's favorite: Found a Peanut. Like most siblings, we would get louder and louder until our giggling fits would inevitably end with a poke or a punch. To discourage random conflicts the elders easily distracted us with a mention of the scenery we were missing: cows, barns, huge trees with Spanish moss, red dirt, fields that went on as far as the eye could see. The South was filled with a multitude of glorious sights uncommon to our surroundings on Long Island; a breathtaking canvas for God's paintings.

We also viewed the small, unpainted clapboard houses that we believed may have once been slave quarters. They must have been a hundred years old, and the ramshackle porches showed evidence people were still living inside them. Not slaves; just poor Americans enduring hardship sanctified with such a beautiful view.

We spent two nights at motels. Large billboards gave warnings for hundreds of miles in advance. We whittled away the time reading the signs and watching the remaining miles decrease. The Southern states had smaller signs on different motels stating white or colored. Mom never showed any – nor tolerated – prejudice in our home and that meant some deli-

cate explanations for Joyce and me. Grandpa didn't necessarily agree with her point of view; the ensuing debates and dialogue made our trip interesting and the ride more bearable.

After three long, amazing days, we reached Florida. Crossing over the state line, we stopped at the welcome station. A woman inside had informational packets about the state along with maps and souvenirs. The best part was when she offered us free orange juice! We all drank up then headed for Pinellas County.

It was the middle of July and paradise. I loved my Grandparent's house, a true Florida style bungalow boasting lots of 1950's style pink and aqua trim. With dusk approaching we inhaled the fragrance of the trees and tropical shrubs. Only a hint of pink was left in the sky, and a balmy breeze kissed our flesh. Stars blinked on, one after another, as the sky turned to the darkest hues of blue.

Joyce was, for the most part, only interested in meeting the sixteen-year-old boy next door. Grandma had already told her of him and thought it would be nice for Joyce to meet someone close to her own age. From the front of our grandparent's house, we tried to catch a glimpse of him through the darkness. Joyce asked me, "Do you think he's cute?" Perhaps I was not the one to ask; after all, I had just completed sixth grade and most of the boys I grew up with still harbored cooties. Peering across the yard and through the window of a dimly lit room, we could see the boy next door with his rather large nose in a book. Not exactly conducive to forming an opinion, I finally said, "I'm not impressed."

I slept in the Florida room, one step up from a screened porch. Our first morning in Florida, we arose early to the sound of a dove's cooing. With sunshine peeking through the curtains, fresh air gently whispered, "Wake up." After breakfast we ventured outdoors to explore our new environment. The sprinklers were on and the smell of wet, green grass was delicious. I knew I was going to like Florida but had no idea that it would feel this heavenly. Grandma had told us it was summer here all year long. My young mind immediately knew I would someday have to live where summer never ends.

We had been outside for only a few minutes when this amazing redheaded woman and her son came over to offer introductions. I met this grown-up as Alberta and at first felt uncomfortable calling an adult by her given name, but my grandma and mom acted as though it was okay. Alberta's son's name was Billy. That July morning when I saw him close up, I noticed Billy's blue eyes with the longest eyelashes ever and his tall, lean body. I liked his haircut and thought there really wasn't anything I didn't like. I never even thought about cooties. As a blush flushed over my face, I found no words were able to form in my mouth. I had never had a feeling quite like this and wasn't sure what it was. I was uncomfortable in this blushing, muted form. Fortunately, Alberta continued to talk and no one noticed the arrow cupid had shot into my heart. All I could do was awkwardly shift my weight from one side of my body to the other as I listened. Shyness kept me from speaking.

At twelve years old, I adored dogs rather than cats and saved babysitting money for clothes. I wore a cross around my neck because I loved Jesus. Until this point I hadn't paid too much attention to how I looked and had only recently come to the realization that mirrors could reflect my changing body. My aunt had told me once I was like a long stemmed rose, which at that moment seemed to fit: long, lanky and very red.

There were times I would stare at my reflection in the mirror and could see I was transforming into a young lady. I was taller than average when comparing myself with other girls my age. My weight had begun to redistribute, rendering my figure adequate. Almost full-grown, I stood 5'4" in my bare feet. I was satisfied with my straight chestnut brown hair and knew that my dad was responsible for my dark brown eyes. Preteen hormones were raging, but jump roping and giggling still gave way to my not-yet-a-woman attitude.

After some conversation with our new neighbors, Billy asked if Joyce and I would like to go to the stock car races with him and his cousin Carol. He had four tickets. Billy and some of his friends had gone to the races the week before and had been rained out. Rain date stubs were good for this week-end. Our mother hesitated at first; Grandma intervened, and mom gave us permission to go.

Billy and his cousin Carol picked us up later that evening in Billy's parents' car, a 1956 Dodge Coronet. This was the first time I had gone anywhere without a grown-up driving. Joyce and I sat in the back seat while Billy drove and Carol got acquainted with my sister and me. When she asked me how old I was, I told her, "Twelve," then verified, "twelve and a half." Billy exclaimed, "You're how old? I thought you were at least fourteen!" Not realizing we were at a stoplight, I gasped as he turned around in the driver's seat to stare at me. Baffled, his action brought my face to a crimson glow. Re-thinking his comment, I smiled with gratitude then melted into the cloth seat. My sister and Carol sensed what was happen-ing and their laughter spontaneously captured the moment. Joyce didn't seem to care that Billy was giving all his atten-tion to her little sister. She could see we were falling in love.

When we arrived at the races, Billy took my hand and helped me climb the bleachers. He didn't let go as we sat watching the races. My whole thought process was mystified and thrilled. Was this like a date? I knew I was too young for a date, yet it was everything I had thought one would be. Somehow, during the races, it was decided that Carol would drive all of us home. Billy and I sat in the back seat and Joyce up front. He put his arm around me and held me close. I had fantasized about someday growing up and having a boyfriend, anticipating it would be like this. I loved this feeling and loved having Billy's arm around my shoulder. As we pulled up the driveway, he didn't release his arm to get out but instead leaned over, his other hand raising my face to his, and tenderly kissed my lips; my first kiss.

That summer love was fun and pure and innocent. We enjoyed being neighbors. With no way of realizing it at the time, we kissed and held hands and captured moments on a continual basis that would last us a lifetime.

I remember so well squeezing each others hands or, when apart – he in his house, I at my Grandma's – we would clap. With the windows open the sounds of our clapping could be easily heard. Clapping or squeezing three times meant, "I love you." The other would reply with two squeezes or claps. This in turn meant, "Mean it?" Then, of course, the reply would be one time, "yes!" We also extended it to four times in a row, and this would mean, "I love you, more!" Sometimes Grandpa would ask, "What are you kids up to?" Our secret squeezes and playful claps conveyed our love repeatedly, and no one else ever knew.

***

Interrupting my thoughts, Stacie said, "Mom, would you check the directions please?" Startled, I picked up the papers on my lap. Northbay Hospital had given us an explicit roadmap to Morton Plant. Stacie said, "This is 580; do I turn here?" We were entering Clearwater, and neither Stacie nor I were accustomed to getting there on our own. Bill usually drove while we all would enjoy the scenery. I looked at the papers, wishing my brain would cooperate. "Yes," I said. "Turn right." The last couple of miles I guided her until we could see a huge hospital complex. We drove into the area shown on the map that said Emergency Room Entrance and a young man walked up to us. Stacie gave him the keys as I gathered my things. Valet parking at a hospital, how ingenious; all we had to do was walk up the sidewalk to the hospital entrance. Shaye and Billy were right behind us, and we all entered into a large room with couches and TVs. A nurse seated at a large desk asked if we needed help. I explained we were meeting with Bill, and he probably should have arrived already.

Bureaucracy in action, he was indeed there, but the paperwork was not ready. We were told to expect a short wait. I had no patience for any wait. I needed to see Bill now. After about one minute I sternly told the nurse behind the desk, "It is imperative we be led to Bill's bedside." I didn't even know at that point if he was still alive. I was near hysteria so the kids took over, and within a few moments we were led through two large doors and down a glistening hallway to a room. The small sign on the door read PRIVATE WAITING ROOM.

Chapter 3

The room was small but accommodated six chairs, two on each of the three walls. End tables with lamps stood in each corner, and a window with a tailored valance was above two of the chairs. Midday sunshine surrendered a stream of light directed to the wall where it pulsated in quick, vibrato moves. The carpeted floor and a few magazines gave it homey feeling, instead of an institutional atmosphere.

The nurse told us to have a seat and said, "The Doctor will be in shortly."

I sat down in one of the arm chairs to the left of the room. The navy blue leather felt cold on my legs. I was wearing shorts for work and hadn't changed. Billy sat down next to me; Stacie and Shaye in the chairs under the window. The door had been shut and we could vaguely hear the hospital sounds from outside the door. We didn't talk. Stacie, Billy, Shaye, and I sat like frigid stones staring at the tiny dancing rivulets of light.

This silence was interrupted when the four of us heard the door knob rattle and watched as it turned. The doctor walked in and appearing to have grave concern introduced himself. "Hello," he paused, closing the door behind him. "I am Doctor Grady." He immediately threw off an aura of distance and seemed very aloof, not warm. He lowered himself into a chair across from the four of us. Words slithered from his mouth. I couldn't relate to his approach. He seemed more like management than a doctor. We all sat there in this cubicle, feeling like the family of number 1000789.

Dr. Grady was a real piece of art. He stood about five feet eleven inches on a medium to small frame. He wore a black suit, white starched shirt and thin black tie. He didn't have a face. Let me clarify that. He had one; it was clean shaven, powerful, with a small thin mouth, dark hair and eyes. I suppose I just couldn't read him; concern yes, empathy no. He kept his emotions tied tight, like his thin black tie. I kept trying to hear what he was saying but only could pick up bits and pieces. My mind was racing, yet the kids seemed particularly intent on each and every word.

I had discriminatory hearing, a condition I'm sure I was born with. The bottom line: Bill would have to have repairs and there was no guarantee. Selectively I interpreted, Bill was still alive. I felt relieved at that moment and went back to watching the small sunbeam that had now found a safe place to perform on the arm of my chair. The kids, who had been listening carefully, did not seem as relieved with what Dr. Grady had said. I took notice of their faces and could see that I needed to understand. I definitely was in what is known as a state of shock. Trying harder, I just couldn't comprehend the mumble jumble pouring from the Doctor's face.

My voice quavered as I asked, "Could you explain one more time? What exactly is a brain aneurysm?"

Dr. Grady probably felt he didn't get paid enough at that point, he replied, "Dr. Lopez will be able to explain that better than I."

Then we were herded to another room and, again, told to wait. Walking down the hall I wondered, *"For what – the other doctor?"* I wanted to see Bill. I wanted to help my husband.

We all followed directions and the children hovered around me with deep concern. The second room had a sign that read 'Radiology Family Area' where other people were waiting, too. My keen sense of our surroundings led me to a large round table where I placed my bag of clothes. I noticed a vending machine at one end of the room. A nurse's station and lots of chairs filled the space. I realized I knew some of the people who were standing around. The kids had already started talking with them. These people were some of mine. How had my brain overlooked my sister Kathie and brother-in-law Dave, my niece Robin, my sister Joyce and her husband Mickey? A few other faces were recognizable. They all headed toward me to reach out with loving arms, tears welling in their eyes.

My reaction was frenzied. Why had everyone showed up as if Bill wasn't going to make it? I hadn't mentally rendez-voused with this scenario and began to cry. I sobbed as they held me tight. As they all took a turn with each of the kids, I began to understand that what was happening was indeed real. This truth I measured for the first time: *I may never see my husband alive again.*

It wasn't long before a young man opened the door wearing one of those papery outfits that surgeons dress in, with tie strings holding everything together and a head covering allowing a little bit of his blond hair to show. He scanned the roomful of people now staring at him and announced, "I am Dr. Lopez. Mrs. Faulkner?"

Everyone else faded away as I stood there alone and answered, "I'm Mrs. Faulkner..." My voice trailed off as he looked at me and began to walk closer. I asked, "Are you taking care of my husband?"

His accent and charisma brought forth a sentiment of trust. "Yes, Mrs. Faulkner." Turning to face everyone, he asked, "Is this your family?" I nodded. "Mrs. Faulkner, we have taken your husband to where we can prepare him for surgery. Your husband has suffered a ruptured brain aneurysm. He has been stabilized and we have three choices. One, we can do nothing at all. The rupture may heal by itself. It may also rupture again in a few days. If this happens your husband will likely not survive.

"Our second choice is to open your husband's skull and repair the artery. We never know how this will affect your husband's mental abilities. He may not survive and, if he does, we would have to wait until he heals and only then we would be able to assess any damage.

"The third choice is to place a coil in the rupture and stop any additional blood flow. This is the least invasive. If Mr. Faulkner can hold on for the next forty-eight hours his chances for survival improve. He still could have severe mental or physical problems. Most likely he will be in the hospital for about a month and a rehabilitation facility for about six months. We won't be sure of any conclusive diagnosis; healing takes up to a year. All we can do is pray for the best. I will need you to sign the consent forms. Do any of you have questions? Would you like a minute to discuss this with your children?"

My children listened intently, nodding their heads in agreement, indicating yes to the coil. I approved surgery to have the coil placed in my husband's brain. Dr. Lopez asked if I would sign the papers he held so he could begin. He motioned to Billy, "Would you get that book on the chair so your mom will have a hard surface to write on?" Billy retrieved the book Dr. Lopez pointed to and handed it to me. It was the Holy Bible I held in my hand. I placed the papers upon it and signed my name; then handed them to Dr. Lopez. I looked him in the eyes and told him, "I have loved this man since I was twelve years old. I will have to trust you. I will place all my faith in you to help him. God bless you."

He looked at me, putting his arm around my shoulder, and with kindness said, "I will do my best."

I asked Dr. Lopez if I would be able to see Bill before the surgery. He said, "No. Your husband is being readied for surgery. The unit is sterile." I would have to wait until the surgery was completed. "I should be finished in about one and a half hours. I'll see you then."

The large clock on the wall read four o'clock. It had been a long day. I wasn't hungry, but I wanted some coffee and a cigarette. The non-smokers said they'd notify us if anything new came up while the kids and I headed out to the smoking area. Knowing that Bill would be in surgery for awhile, we could take a deep breath and attempt to slow the uncontrolled momentum of this runaway train we were riding.

The heat of the sun still remained, and it felt good to feel the warmth since inside the hospital it was very cold. A table for four was available in the far corner of the patio. Stacie coughed suspiciously as we headed past the others who had gathered for a smoke. I was glad at least one of my kids didn't smoke. We sat down and, like a switch that had been turned on, they all began speaking at once.

Billy said, "I prayed during the long ride down here that Dad would live. Dad hasn't finished teaching me everything I need to know."

Stacie expressed her feelings about the first room we had been led to. She thanked God that Dr. Grady didn't have to tell us Dad was gone. Shaye and Billy agreed. They had watched too much television to know what happens when the family is led to a private room to wait for the doctor.

We all got a little giddy for a few minutes as the adrenalin in our bodies began to defrost. I wondered why something like this has to happen for everyone to cling tight to one another. I was so proud of my children; our children. Fright had only lessened momentarily, though, and then it came back. The world felt so huge. I felt so small. I felt so lost. I numbly sat drinking my coffee and finishing my second or third cigarette.

That's when I noticed a stranger staring at us. Continuing their conversations, the kids seemed to be singing a love song to their Dad. I wasn't grasping all that was being said, yet appreciated their presence. I glanced back to the stranger and realized how alone he appeared. He sat in one of the patio chairs and seemed to be eavesdropping on our family. I knew how desperate I felt and found myself trying to imagine what I would be feeling if I were alone during all this. I looked at him one more time. He had beautiful blue eyes; the color of my Bill's when we were in the pool. His frame was medium and his tawny skin wrinkled. His eyes had shown that tears were lingering, being held back by his own weakening strength. One man alone; I wondered why he was here at this hospital. Was his suffering equal to mine? Oh, God, if it were – how could he do this alone? I knew the kids wondered what I was up to, but I felt compelled to introduce myself.

"My name is Valerie." I reached out my hand and said, "Would you like to join us? I don't think we will be great company, but you can pull up a chair. You can set your coffee on our table."

"Oh, no thank you, ma'am. I'm fine." Just a small curve of his mouth revealed he appreciated the gesture. I had tried. I didn't regret trying. The kids seemed puzzled. Then figured it was their cue to get me food.

Stacie asked, "Mom, have you eaten today?"

"No, not yet, I haven't had a chance."

"Well, how about we find the cafeteria?"

"Just give me a few more minutes, honey. Okay? Thank you all for being here for me. I love you all so much."

Shaye reached over and took my hand. I held tight and struggled to hold back the tears. I muttered, "Could we say a prayer before we go back in? Shaye, could you help?" We all held hands and listened as Shaye softly spoke.

"Heavenly Father, we pray that you will sustain us. Allow our faith to prevail. Please, Lord, heal Dad so that he will be whole again and even better than he was before. Wrap your loving arms around us, and touch your healing hands to his body. Give this hospital and its doctors the knowledge to perform the tasks necessary. Father we praise you and glorify you. In your holy name, we pray. Amen."

"Amen."

"Amen."

"Amen."

Chapter 4

The clock kept ticking as five-thirty came and went. I wanted to believe that no news was good news, but this was not the time for that. I paced up and down. Nothing could stop this anxious feeling that controlled me. Five minutes would slowly pass; then five more. After smoking till my lungs hurt and drinking coffee until my stomach ached, I found refuge in the bathroom. I felt faint and found the endless quivering unbearable. Standing at the sink counter, I summoned God. "Have Dr. Lopez return soon, or I will die. Please, God, give him the brilliance to do this right, please. Oh, and God, if Dr. Lopez was not at the head of the class....please allow him do A-plus work." I couldn't believe what I was saying as I cried out loud. I looked up at myself in the mirror. I hadn't accepted that this day was bona fide. Looking at the tired, weary, frightened stranger staring back at me, I realized I had to face the facts; this was indeed certainty. Sobbing I had one more appeal: "Please, Lord...Please. I can't take this anymore. God, I need a miracle!"

My sister Joyce came in to check on me. With tissues covering my face I could hide from that translucent reflective image, but my voice disclosed the truth. "What time is it?" I asked, sniffling. She said, "Come out by the family; it won't be long." She reached to take my hand and walked me out.

The clock was passing six-thirty, more than an hour after my expectations. I stared down the hallway where Bill was still in surgery. I squeezed my tissue-filled hands and strolled back to a chair to collapse. The clock ticked on and on. It was nearly seven o'clock p.m. when Dr. Grady, very businesslike, walked in. He obviously wasn't wearing scrubs. I didn't know what to expect. He asked, "Has Dr. Lopez been here yet?"

As he spoke, Dr. Lopez came through the door. "I'm sorry it took so long," he said. "The coil is in and the bleeding has stopped. Your husband is in recovery and…"

I had jumped up and ran to him. I put my arms around him and hugged him tight. "Thank you, thank you. Can I see him?" I included Dr. Grady and without hesitation gave him a big hug, too. Dr. Grady's mannerisms relayed a message that he would have preferred not to have total strangers hugging him.

Dr. Lopez continued, "Yes, Mrs. Faulkner. Go through those doors and follow the directions to the Intensive Care Unit. He should be there now."

The elevator ride led all of us to the ICU. The doors opened to an empty hallway, wide and clear, although not very long. No obstacles; only the paint on the walls and bright florescent lights overhead. There were two very large doors with a sign that read "DO NOT ENTER." To one side of the hall laid a room with a window and door that read "Family Sitting Area." We entered to find chairs, a couch, a TV, and several magazines. In the corner sat a telephone with a placard which explicitly read, "CALL FIRST FOR PERMISSION TO ENTER THE ICU." After dialing the number listed, the answering nurse said I could enter the unit and gave me directions to Bill's room. I relayed this to the kids and Stacie said, "Go ahead, Mom. We'll give you a minute alone."

As I pushed the automatic door button, my heart beat heavily as the two large doors slowly swung open. The floors were glistening; everything looked immaculately clean. I was to go down another hall, then turn right. Bill's room would be directly across from the nurse's station. Walking into the unknown was frightening. With fear weighing gravely upon me,

I could actually feel the beating thumps of my heart pounding in my chest.

I passed about four rooms. Each area hosted an elderly patient with equipment surrounding their beds. Beeping sounds and noises were apparent as I passed each space, briefly diminishing as I continued my journey. The patients all seemed to be sleeping, or maybe it was the swishing sounds of the air machines that sounded like snoring. A desk and chair placed outside each room were fitted with compartments for holding medical charts and files. I had never been in an ICU. I felt small and fragile as though I were being swallowed up by a huge monster. Ahead I could see the nurse's station. I was told the room directly across the hall was Bill's.

There he lay, motionless. He appeared to be the youngest patient in the unit. The hours I had spent waiting and wondering seemed surreal. Bill's head was not wrapped up in bandages like I'd expected. He actually looked relaxed and very handsome. At 59 years old he had only a few strands of gray hair. His face smooth, he really had no signs of fatigue. And his coloring was remarkably good.

A sudden flash of how my mother-in-law looked as she lay in her coffin at her funeral sent chills down my spine. She looked so beautiful yet, when someone has died, it really doesn't seem to matter how good they look; they're dead after all. In an eerie kind of way that's how Bill looked. My eyes immediately went to his chest to see the ups and downs that occur when someone is breathing. The movement was slow and steady. I whispered, "Thank God." Then I could see that a machine brought air to his body and then released it. My husband was dependent on a machine? Bill had always read science-fiction books and often would share what he had read. This felt like something he had told me about once. Probably about futuristic machinery and the like: machines, working to keep the body alive, with lots of wires and tubes going into his body. But where was he, his mind, the person I knew? Dr.

Lopez said he would probably not be able to speak. I rationalized his statement.

He had a crisp white sheet over him, and I wasn't sure at first if I should touch him. He and everything in the room was so sterile. When the nurse came in, I introduced myself. Whispering I asked, "May I touch him?" She assured me in a normal speaking voice that it was okay to touch him, but since he was in a coma not to expect any response.

Whispering slightly louder, I responded, "Coma?" I immediately stroked his hand, then his arm. I again whispered, "Bill?" When Bill slept at home just the lightest touch could awaken him. Here, now... nothing. His body just laid there, no sensation of awareness. "Bill, I'm here."

I heard somewhere that people in comas can hear, so I quietly spoke, repeating, "I'm here, honey." I stroked his listless arm. Tears momentarily fogged my vision and a lump formed in my throat. I prayed quietly, "Please, God, keep Bill comfortable and free of pain. Please, Bill, hear me. Please give me a sign, anything, that... Bill? Sweetheart...?"

Since only two visitors at a time were allowed in the room, the kids shared their time with one another. I remained in the room and with a whisper would recognize each child and tell Bill who was there. I sat by his bed for the next few hours. I didn't know exactly what to say to the nurses, leaving conversation brief. I needed knowledge and would ask what was happening, but generally they had their jobs to do and interruptions were not appreciated. As the staff passed in and out of the room, I realized I was watching a well-rehearsed ballet, and each performer knew his or her roll to perfection.

The clock endlessly kept ticking. Minutes became hours and time marched on. The doctors had warned me that Bill's condition was life-threatening, and the first forty-eight hours could be his last. The longer he fought, the better his chances for survival; precious time bringing us closer to what could be ahead of us. I clung to each moment like a delicacy to be savored and cherished. I had no clue what the future would be like. Bill had always said, *"When life sometimes has its valleys... this day, too, shall end."* I always felt optimistic when I related to his theory; sure life would be better tomorrow. But I was clinging to today. As horrid as it was, I feared tomorrow more. Today, Bill was alive.

Chapter 5

"Mom, are you awake?" I heard a gentle rap on my bedroom door. "Mom, do you want to come downstairs and have some coffee?" Billy had stayed the night with me and was up already.

"Shit, it's seven forty-five!" I sat on the edge of the bed. *Oh, God, I've been rolled over by a tank. I need to get to the hospital. I have to hurry. Where are my jeans? I still have stuff in that bag. Got to brush my teeth.* I thought about what he had said and replied, "Yes, I'll be down in a minute." *I'll get dressed in a little bit I need some coffee first.* I hobbled downstairs as Jake followed.

"Morning, Mom. Sleep okay? Stacie and Shaye are coming soon and are going to help."

He was still such a morning person. Jake followed me outside where I sat at the porch table. I needed to wake up. *Bill's not here.* What was I going to do? I needed to cancel scheduled work and pay some bills and get to Morton Plant Hospital at least two hours ago. Billy brought coffee, which he usually doesn't drink, out for the both of us and gave me a hug and a mug. He could see I was upset and, as if he already knew what I had been thinking, said, "Don't worry, Mom. We'll get some stuff done and be down in Clearwater by noon."

"Noon, no, we have to leave right now!" He didn't even flinch as he listened to me, easily seeing I was still in my bathrobe.

"Mom, don't you remember? The nurse said not to come too early. Dad has to get a lot of tests done, and he won't even be in his room."

I thought about what Billy said. Then remembered what the nurse had told us just last night. Maybe ten hours ago.

"Okay, yeah. I remember now."

It seemed my mind was not working too well. I just needed to settle down and take one thing at a time. I took another sip of coffee and told Billy, "I'm going to go take a shower and get dressed. Holler if your sisters get here before I get out."

"I will. Take your time. We have a couple hours."

I let the water run to heat up, something Bill always did, and placed a towel in reach. The warmth of the shower felt good, but I couldn't hold back my tears. I was so alone. I felt hopelessly dependant on Bill and so totally lost without him. My life surreal, I couldn't imagine when I was just me. I tried to remember.

***

In 1967, I was young and spirited. My parents had taught me that faith, hard work and independence were characteristics I should achieve. I felt like the world and my future were pages in a book just waiting to be turned. I was a senior and enjoying my last year of high school. Where I would be after graduation was not clear; I just knew I desired the 'road less traveled' and, at seventeen, would enjoy life and live in the moment. The days, weeks, and months had been filled with long-awaited 'lasts,' last homecoming football game, last mid-term exams, and last time I had to ride a bus.

I'd saved babysitting money and allowance for quite

some time. Thanksgiving weekend a local radio station broadcasted 'Pinch Penny News,' where locals could sell their wares over the air. I hadn't really been paying too much attention until I heard the last caller. A gentleman described his 1951 Cadillac in fair running condition. It would need tires but would surely be a steal for fifty dollars. He left his phone number as the Pinch Penny jingle ended the show. Jumping up and down, I screeched, "Mom! Mom! Did you hear that? I have fifty dollars! Please, please may I call? Can we go see the 1951 Cadillac? Please?"

My parents couldn't imagine what kind of condition a fifty dollar car could be in, but after pleading diligently and promising to accept extra duties for the privilege of even looking, they agreed. I overflowed with anticipation as we turned into the gentleman's driveway. At 17, anyone over 30 seemed relatively old, and the man coming out the door to greet us was just that. With dark wavy hair, he stood tall in his overalls and flannel shirt. Pulling a sweater over his head, he walked toward us. When his arms popped out of his cuffs, I could see that he held a key in his hand. "There she is." About 100 feet away, next to an old barn, my freedom beckoned.

Leaves covered the dull gray finish, making it look like a camouflaged army tank. As we walked, he praised her with affectionate poetry. She had been his first. "She has charm for her age! Automatic transmission, radiant heat that will keep you toasty and, well, she does guzzle the gas, but overall she's faithful and will never let you down."

He handed me the keys to unlock the door. Creaky noises followed as I slowly forced the door open. Examining the front seat, I brushed off the dust and thought to myself, "Old girl, you're perfect." Mom struggled to get in the passenger side as I started the engine. She fiddled with the heat and radio controls; all those luxurious, custom extras which seemed in working condition.

I shifted into drive and proceeded slowly around the open field ahead. She was very big yet purred like a kitten. I started to turn her around and found her one flaw. With no power steering, I struggled as I attempted to turn. Letting up on the gas, she obliged like a stubborn old mule that had been persuaded by a sugar cube.

My Caddie was about 20 feet long, and I needed a ladder to reach the middle of the roof. The automatic radio antenna disappeared into her hood when I pushed a toggle switch and would come back out when I pushed it again. She seemed to have so many buttons, each entertained me with amazement. Even my parents had not known such technology in their much newer vehicles. Radiant heat warmly conveyed from underneath the front seat. Most cars back then had a rear window shelf. I could have stretched out on hers for a nap, and her trunk was practically like another room. She sported white-walled tires with huge inscribed hubcaps reading Cadillac.

I was having the time of my life. Christmas break would begin soon, and for two weeks I could drive around the world, figuratively speaking.

The school bell rang and I headed out to my car. My mood was exhilarating to say the least. I arrived home that afternoon, kicked off my shoes, dropped my books, and headed for the refrigerator. Mom greeted me and she, too, appeared to be in a rather exuberant mood.

"Guess what?" She grinned from ear to ear. "We're leaving on the 20th when you finish your last day of school and having Christmas in Florida. Grandma and Grandpa are thrilled! They just can't face the snow this year."

"What? Wait – I can't go to Florida! I have plans, my friends." I began whining, "Mom, we all know it wouldn't feel like Christmas." I slammed the refrigerator door shouting,

"You're ruining my life! You go and I'll stay home. I'm 17, you know; I have my own car and can take care of myself." Mom cut me off with out the slightest consideration.

"We're going and you are going with us!"

Her sudden change in attitude left me speechless. Her grin had turned downward with disappointment. Thinking, I realized I should have been more tactful but instead had been arrogant and defiant. In my own defense, I sweetly motioned as though to get one more word in, but she abruptly pointed at me and said, "We're going." She turned to walk away and deliberately mumbled, "Billy will be home on leave from the Navy," then continued, ' Grandma and Grandpa are so excited. I'm excited! I need a break from this business, and I want to see the sun."

Mom went on and on, but all I kept hearing was, "Billy will be there." It had been three years since I saw him last, when I was 14 and he was 19 – too much of an age difference. But now I was 17. That would make him...22? He was my first love. Had I heard her correctly? I stared at Mom, desperately attempting to ignore the warm feeling emerging on my cheeks, as I as nonchalantly as possible rephrased her comment. "Did you say Billy would be there, too?"

In response to my flippant attitude, she answered sarcastically, "Yes."

The thought of seeing him was definitely intriguing. I added up the years and was certain he was twenty-two years old. The rest of the week I wondered if any element of our summer love could be present after so many years. I pondered the thought as the December 20th grew closer. Keeping my seventeen-year-old character in line, I had to limit my excitement quota to the privacy of my own room. There I listened to rock-and-roll and thumbed through the old photographs, memories waltzing through my head. Retying the pink shoelace that had held my keepsakes together, I thought, "This is too crazy. I've watched too many Twilight Zones," as the musical theme echoed through my mind.

About three days before Christmas, we arrived in Florida. My Mom and Dad were happy to have a break from the northern weather and already were making plans to do some fun things. My agenda read: stop thinking about the boy next door. Early the next morning, Bill arrived. He and his parents came over to welcome us to Florida. I could hear them outside and hurried to finish dressing. They were standing by the front door talking to my parents. As I came out to meet them, my eyes met Bill's. My face began to blush and I knew Cupid was back. Obviously his arrow plunged into both of our hearts. Had what was once a lost summer love, long ago, reawakened? Was this destiny?

The Florida weather was Chamber of Commerce perfect, and on such a beautiful day Bill asked if I had plans. Would I like to go to the beach with him? The beach! I remembered the summer of sixty-two when Bill, my sister, and I went to the beach almost every day. My Grandma would drive us the few miles to the water's edge, and we would spend the day enjoying the warm water and white sand. I couldn't wait.

Bill picked me up in his red sports car, and with the top down we headed to Redington Beach. In 1967, Redington Beach was a conglomeration of private homes and small motels with open beach front dividing the buildings. Bill pulled up to a section of beach where there was public access to the Gulf of Mexico. We parked the car and with our blankets and towels headed across the sand. Although the day was warm, the Gulf water temperature was still too chilly to go swimming. We spent that afternoon catching up on what had been happening in our lives. Bill told me about life aboard an aircraft carrier, and I brought him up to date with high school and the things going on in my hometown.

We stayed there and watched the sun turn from yellow to orange to fiery red as it set into the west, diving deep into the blue Gulf waters. Just as the sun dipped below the horizon, Bill took me into his arms and gently kissed me. I felt like Cinderella. I kissed him as we held each other, and he kissed me. Neither of us had forgotten; puppy love had just grown up.

Eventually, we packed up our towels and headed back to the car. Bill took my hand in his as we walked through the sand. Holding his hand felt so right. Just before we reached the car, he squeezed my hand three times. I stopped in the sand and looked up at him. Without hesitation I replied by squeezing twice, and he squeezed once more. We both felt the connection that comes when two people are, without question, twin souls.

***

The shower started to run cold just as Billy yelled, "Mom! Stacie's here."

Chapter 6

Stacie, Billy, and I arrived at the hospital at noon. Shaye was on a roller coaster timeline at work. Hired as a graphic artist, she couldn't hold up the presses. She needed just an extra hour to make her deadline and told us she would meet us at the hospital. She totally understood the 'ants in my pants' and that I was concerned and needed to leave. I totally understood her situation. Her boss had been good to her. She couldn't ignore this particular deadline. It was that important.

There had been needless worry. Bill was not back from having tests. While we were sitting in the ICU waiting area, a woman came in, seeming rather pleased she had actually found us. Her identification badge disclosed her mission as Medical Assistant. Thankfully, with Stacie's help, the paperwork didn't take too long. I explained, "We don't have medical insurance. We'll need to make payments. We do pay our bills," I promised.

She then advised, "That is why I'm here to help. In situations like this, one of your first tasks should be to notify the Social Security Administration." Stacie asked all the right questions and even I was beginning to connect the dots. To summarize: we needed to apply early for disability and/or death benefits.

I wasn't prepared for this. I had actually felt blessed during the morning hours as I watched my family. The bittersweet notion of having my kids in the same place at the same time and admiring how they kept our family together had actually brought some peace to me. This lady couldn't have expected me to listen to all of this and not become upset. I really needed to keep my faith and hope strong, and she was not conducive to either. Her empathetic tone of voice wasn't accomplishing her task; I despised her words. "Mrs. Faulkner, I know this is hard for you. But I have seen so many cases like this and your husband, if he survives, more than likely will need rehabilitation. He may never work again. Funds are available through the State and Federal Government."

I contemplated that thought and surmised if Bill didn't work I, too, would not be able to. My job depended on him. *I depended on him.* Swallowing, I listened to my inner voice. *"Val,"* it said, *"this has to be the worst day of your life. Your husband is in critical condition. You can't go see him. Chances are statistically in your favor that you are most likely going to end up old, broke and alone. Like a bag lady pushing a shopping cart? Wait a minute, Val – let's not get carried away – at least, not yet."* I was staring, but I hadn't intended to make her feel uncomfortable. When I announced I needed to get some fresh air, the woman quickly and very politely responded, "That's fine. We're done for now. Take care, Mrs. Faulkner."

For the next couple hours we meandered around, waiting for the ICU to let us in. Excuses, one after another, seemed to be wasting precious moments. We made the trek down to the first floor numerous times. I kept getting lost, my sense of direction off balance until Billy said calmly, "Mom, there are signs everywhere. Look, the cafeteria has a blue directional arrow. Now follow the blue line on the floor. It will take you right there." It appeared there were colored paths inlaid in the linoleum. Guess it never took much to please me, so I gave him a great big hug in appreciation. I marveled at Billy's awareness to have figured that out already and wondered why I hadn't. This new bit of information definitely helped. I now was able to maneuver around the hallways like a pro, the directional borders discretely guiding my every step.

Finally, at about two-thirty in the afternoon, Bill was back in his quarters. Shaye had arrived and she and I entered the ICU together. Stacie and Billy would wait to take a turn. It had already felt like such a long day. Each apprehensive step brought us closer to his area. The curtain was pulled closed. I strained to see through the slits and could see someone inside. Shaye and I clasped hands as we stood there in expectation. Without saying a word we waited.

Then the plastic clips clacked on the curtain rod as it slid open. Dr. Grady, in his suit, came out. He acknowledged us and said, "Mrs. Faulkner, Mr. Faulkner is stable. The tests show the bleeding is under control. Possibly tomorrow we will attempt to bring him out of the induced coma, questions?" Before I could answer he finished. "Fine, we will see you tomorrow." He turned away from Shaye and me and began writing in the chart outside Bill's room. Shaye and I were both stunned. We were not prepared for him. The brief confrontation with 'The Suit' had just left us dumbfounded and speechless.

As I numbly adjusted Bill's sheet I thought of all I'd been bombarded with this day; the Medical Assistance lady, the multi-colored floor lines, 'The Suit.' Then, as though replayed in my brain, I heard, *induced coma!*

I knew what a coma was. I actually was in a coma when I was two years old. Back in 1952, the doctors had told my parents I probably wouldn't make it. Spinal Meningitis was deadly, and when it gets to the coma stage, one generally doesn't wake up. My family always told me I must have been kissed by an angel. I abruptly turned to speak to Dr. Grady, but he had already left. Frustrated, I didn't like the way that man made me feel. His intellectual aura somehow made me feel insignificant, unequal. Nobody should be able to do that. I stared at Bill. He was in the same spot as the night before. My kisses, my voice, nothing could interrupt his lifeless sleep. I looked around and wondered what the different machines were doing. Without a doubt in my mind, I knew I needed knowledge. I needed to understand something, *anything,* about this whole new alien world Bill had traveled to. Attempting to conjure up an attitude of significance, right at that moment I decided I would begin my fact-finding mission. Me and God; we would not give up.

The nurses attending to Bill came in constantly. As each one arrived we would shuffle around the stage and then return to our seats. The kids, too, exchanged places every half hour or so. I remained by Bill's side as the day passed. I inwardly chuckled as I watched my son. Billy, having been separated from his wife for over a year, appeared distracted by the stream of beautiful, educated young women. He made me imagine that if my Bill only knew he, too, would have difficulty not staring. I had to smack big Bill on a few occasions in the past when he had rubbernecked, and this too made matters confusing. Where was he? Was he able to sense anyone was there? Did he know I was there?

Shifts changed. As I met more and more of the staff, I asked lots and lots of questions. For the most part I was given direct and adequate answers. One nurse in particular, her name was Michelle, explained to me what an induced coma was and what I could expect over the next few days. She explained, "When someone has a brain injury, like your husband's, medications are given to simulate a coma. This in laymen's terms is like a deep sleep. Brain aneurysms allow blood to break through the artery wall and the blood spills where it is not supposed to. The blood in turn distorts and scrambles one's mind and confuses reasoning capabilities. It can damage brain cells and promote strange consequences." She replaced a bag on the I.V. and continued, "Usually meds are delivered for a few days to keep the patient as comfortable and calm as possible. Slowly the amounts are decreased, and under constant supervision the patient is brought back to consciousness. The brain has to be able to understand some instruction before this can happen because some of the tubes –

like the breathing tube – can easily be removed as long as there is patient cooperation. Do you understand what I'm saying?"

"Yes." I had been trying to put my hand in Bill's. "Thank you, Michelle. Really, you are a good teacher. I appreciate the explanation. I think I just will need a little more time to absorb all this."

Six o'clock came and, although visiting hours were over, I lingered a bit longer. I remembered the kids had families, too, and they more than likely were ready to go home. What a long day. I kissed Bill goodbye. "I love you, Bill. Goodnight."

***

At the Fireplace

In front of the fireplace I looked up at the clock. I'd been going over my notes for over an hour, yet felt compelled to continue on. I thought as I looked up from my papers, "Wow, I really remember that night!" My legs were stiff from sitting Indian style on the tile floor. "Gees, what am I doing? God, do you have a plan?" Glancing down again, the sentence, 'I will just need a little more time to absorb this,' was flashing at me as though an emergency light had gone off in my head. I can't fathom, let alone absorb, any of this. I'm not a writer; I never held the desire to write a novel. I felt like a fish out of water at that writer's association meeting. I don't even like to read books! "God, I know I made a promise, but perhaps you picked the wrong person for this job."

Chapter 7

Darkness surrendered as daylight exposed the morning, revealing sparkling dewdrops and a fine mist serenely blanketing the water. A few birds were ready for song, and the smell of the perking coffee drifted through the kitchen window. Day three, May 11th was our thirty-seventh wedding anniversary. Of course this was not the way I had imagined it to be, but nevertheless, I had a reason to get up early. I planned to gather some photographs together of Bill and me from when we met in 1962, right up through the present. I wanted to present a show and tell tale about us and hoped to place them on a bare wall in his ICU room. I had already made a card for him and piled up the sweet get well drawings the grandkids had done in crayon. There were about ten papers to hang up. Billy had drawn a Cross with sunrays shining in the background. Delicate flowers surrounded the base. I wanted to find a special spot on one of the walls for his drawing.

I couldn't help being optimistic remembering what Dr. Grady had said, that maybe today they would wake up Bill. Surely that would be the best way I could spend this special day. God had delivered such a beautiful morning, and my spirits were a little more hopeful.

By eight o'clock the phone was ringing. Family and business associates wanted a rundown on the latest news and, of course, wanted to send their get well wishes. I repeated the scenario over and over and begged only that a prayer be said to help Bill and me. I held tightly to my faith that, with so many prayers going out to our Heavenly Father, he would hear and life would somehow return to normal.

Innately, the kids seemed to want to stay close to me. I can only imagine that they already suspected this particular day, our anniversary, may be harder on me than I could have expected. Changing the already routine schedule, we began our drive down to the hospital early enough to stop first at a little restaurant called Caposey's for breakfast. Bill and I had recently started eating there after hearing that the food was good, and the kids agreed. The owner welcomed us like old friends. She and her staff hadn't heard about Bill, but some of the fellow patrons – not to my surprise – had. News in a small town travels fast, especially since Bill was so well known and respected in the community. With over thirty years in business, he had also taught in the electrical apprenticeship programs that Pasco and Pinellas Counties had offered. Add church, city government, and half a dozen affiliations – he really had an array of acquaintances. The news had spread like lightning. I wasn't prepared emotionally for face-to-face confrontations so the kids helped me out by explaining the details, and then we sat down.

It wasn't long before I could feel the tears building inside my eyes. No one could have known a large stack of pancakes with a little sprig of parsley could bring a flood of memories roaring into my mind. I always gave Bill the unwanted garnish. He would playfully throw his at my plate because he didn't want it either. I was trying so hard not to let my emotions show, but after all, this was not the way it was supposed to be. One thing led to another, and I decided to get the folder I had prepared for Bill's room to show the waitresses, rather than verbally explain our story. Seeing the sympathetic emotion in their expressions, I felt I could depend on them.

"Please, could you all say a prayer today?" Without hesitation they assured me they would. A hug sealed the request, and for a moment my spirits were again significantly lifted.

***

It wasn't long before I was taping each picture to the wall, all the while talking to Bill. He lay there just as he had for the past two days. I turned to give him a kiss and promised him that God would be there for us. "Our Lord has given us so many blessings honey, and so many people are praying." I squeezed his hand three times hoping for the response I knew could not be returned, then whispered, "It's all right; I'll wait."

Minutes became hours and it seemed the nurses were having even more tasks to do for Bill. Every time they needed to check Bill, I was asked to step out into the hallway. Being juggled in and out of the room, I hovered more and more each time I returned. Praying, talking, and touching him as the equipment hissed and beeped, I wondered when the doctors would come in and release Bill from his unnatural sleep.

When one last test was scheduled and we were told it would be about an hour long, we filed down the corridor paths two by two. Outside we could talk and enjoy the needed fresh air. The hospital surroundings were beginning to seem more familiar. Some people, as well, were less like strangers. The cafeteria people would attempt to make me smile; I tried. I began giving respectful nods to the forlorn man who sat in his usual spot on the smokers' patio.

Watching the kids, I could see they, too, were feeling such pain. They had been so supportive; I wished I could be stronger for them. Making an attempt, I began, "Did I tell you about my Christmas earrings? Dad said he wanted to get me diamonds this year for a special anniversary and Mother's Day gift, but when he saw these he couldn't wait." I pointed to my ears, "He bought them and gave them to me for Christmas."

With a quick wipe of my eyes, I sat up a little taller, clearing my throat. "Ahem. We all need to tell everyone we know to pray for Dad. I know it's hard asking everyone all the time. We need to do this...we can't try to do this all on our own. We need God's help. Please?" Hearing their assurances, I realized I loved them all more than I had known. "Thank you. You guys are the best."

Stacie, Billy, and Shaye continued their conversation while I took a few minutes to sit quietly with my own thoughts. *Thirty-seven wonderful years.* I had been blessed with so much in my life. I twisted the diamond earring in my left ear and thought about how excited I had been opening up the present. I remembered the same feeling on my eighteenth birthday.

***

Bill and I knew we wanted to be together for the rest of our lives. We promised our love to one another during the holidays, and realized that over a six year period, our courtship had actually existed for about six weeks. Still, we felt totally secure promising ourselves to one another.

I was back at school and trying to survive the cold weather on Long Island while he was stationed at Whidbey Island, Washington Navel Air Station. We wrote letters back and forth exploring deeper into our souls. We learned a lot about each other that way and kept growing more and more in love. Just about one week prior to my 18th birthday, a brown cardboard box arrived with the mail. It was a large box, two feet by two feet, addressed to me, and the dented corners proved it had traveled a long way to get to Yaphank. I placed it on the kitchen table and brought a knife to cut through the clear tape that held the box securely closed. Lifting the four flaps, I discovered a letter. Bill wrote 'Happy birthday, sweetheart.' He instructed that since I had already opened the package, I could, in fact, look at, feel and try on everything he had sent even if it were not my birthday. How-

ever, the smaller gift-wrapped box placed inside I would have to wait to open until he called me on my actual birthday at about 6:00 o'clock EST. This seemed fair enough.

I examined the contents immediately. How wonderful! I loved the authentic navy issue, bell bottom jeans, blue denim long sleeve shirt and white sailor hat. Last, the blue denim jacket with Navy Squadron patches and embroidered over the front pocket, 'Faulkner.' I ran to try everything on and truly believed that if I stuck all my hair up inside the sailor hat I could stow away on the ship with Bill and sail the oceans with my love. God, I was so goofy then. All dressed up, I went back to the box and found a bunch of newspaper and heaving one crumpled piece after the other, I found a small package, wrapped and tied with a bow. It was about four inches square, and I felt somewhat disappointed as I thought to myself, "This is not a ring box." I couldn't open it anyway so I went back to the mirror to check out my uniform. My mom found me stuffing my hair up inside the hat and giggled, "I don't think you'll be able to stowaway." With camera in hand she clicked at me as I modeled my new outfit and grabbing her hand, led her to see my other package. We both went back to the kitchen to examine it closer. She knew what I hoped would be inside, but agreed this was not the right size box. I would have to wait. Each day passed and curiosity was about to kill me. Innocently enough I touched, squeezed, and shook the box a number of times every day. I mostly stared at it, as though it would reveal itself to me. Nothing worked and my patience was wearing thin. Then, two days before my birthday I grasped the box and shook it really hard. A muffled tinkle could be heard. I tried that one more time. Again the sound replayed. It was not like the sound of a ring but more like a part of something else. I dreaded the awaited phone call. I would have to explain I had broken the gift. The secret gift Bill had sent, the special gift that I had to refrain from opening until he called on my birthday. What had I done? Nervously I waited and like every other year, finally my day ar-

rived. At exactly 6:00 o'clock the phone rang. On the second ring I answered, "Hello?"

Sounding far away, like long distance sounded back then, a voice, a wonderful voice replied, "Val?

"Yes it's me. Hi honey, Bill?"

A slight echo followed his voice. Bill wished me a happy birthday and asked if my present had arrived. I told him how much I loved the outfit, and he prodded me to find out if I had looked inside the smaller box. I assured him I hadn't but just as I was going to explain I may have broken what was inside he said, "Val, do you love me?"

"Yes, with all my heart."

"Do you want to marry me?"

"Yes, yes!"

"You can open the package."

I tore through the paper while holding the phone on my shoulder and opened the box. Inside, a beautiful diamond ring had merely fallen off the holder.

"I love it; it's beautiful, thank you! I love you." I placed the ring on my finger. "It fits."

So with three thousand miles between us, we were engaged.

***

I hadn't seen Dr. Grady or Dr. Lopez. It was late afternoon when a new doctor arrived. He stopped short in his own tracks when he observed the pictures on the wall. "Oh, wow! What a great idea," he commented. Looking at the photo from 1962, he realized immediately that the two of us went back a long time. "You have definitely humanized your husband; what a great story line. I like the Jeep. Oh, and your wedding picture. Your husband was in the Navy?"

I was pleased with his comments and answered him courteously. We continued with our small talk for a bit longer when he said, "I'm sorry, but we are going to keep Mr. Faulkner induced for a while longer. He needs to recuperate and new tests are showing signs of pneumonia. Sedation and very strong antibiotics will be administered through a pick line. I will need permission to do this. Basically, this line will go deep into the vein and cannot be easily dislodged. All the meds can go through it and we won't need to keep replacing the IV's. Obviously there is always risk involved, so we need you to sign, but..."

He could see I was having trouble with this latest development. I wasn't accepting that Bill couldn't be awakened. Being told about the pneumonia was frightening me.

"How did this happen?" I cried. "How did he get pneumonia in here – of all places?" My body started to tremble again. Things couldn't be worse. It wasn't even forty-eight hours since the surgery, and I wasn't sure he would survive – not now. Not with this.

Chapter 8

My lying in bed unable to sleep made the night seem to go on forever. My brain kept going over and over the past few days. Just thinking became a horrible activity. I wished I could sign out on a timecard and take a vacation from my own thoughts. Experiencing the trauma over and over was so frightening. My faith was strong, but it needed reassurance. God couldn't let Bill die. I couldn't bear to be alone. I needed him. Instead of counting sheep I repeated out loud again and again, "I need to trust; I must."

Not even that worked. I had been lying awake for what seemed forever, trying to sleep. If I dozed off, my slightest movement would awaken me. Hour after hour I got up, and Jake would follow me downstairs. More than once I'd get a glass of milk for myself and some water for him. I talked to him, for I knew he definitely sensed that something seemed strangely different, yet he couldn't be expected to understand. Still, Jake's sad eyes were so compassionate. He attentively watched as I repeatedly called down to the hospital. After about the fourth call the nurse on duty convinced me that Bill was the same as he had been from all the previous calls, and I really should get some needed rest. I had used up my second, third and fourth winds; I decided I had better take someone's advice before morning approached.

I needed to hold on tight, even to the slimmest thread of hope and believe in our Lord's promise. For so many years I had asked for blessings for my family and anyone else I knew. Mom had taught me that when I was very little. Talking to God was something I did every day. I've heard of an expression, a name for people who pray for others: Prayer Warrior, I have to admit I did consider it an honor to be one.

At the side of my bed, I fell to my knees and spoke to God. "Thank you, God, for the wonderful life you have given me. I know I have been really nagging you the past few days, but Lord, please? Just hear me tonight. Could you please just place your loving arms around Bill? Please take care of him and give him the strength to heal and come back home. Thank you, Father." I believed that talking to God was the only way I would find comfort. Afterwards, I actually did feel a renewed inner peace returning to my being and drifted off to sleep.

***

The house was so very quiet except for Jake's snoring. He was sound asleep on his doggy bed. It wasn't any surprise to me that the clock read nine. It must have been about four when I finally fell back to sleep. I counted up the hours with my fingers. Five, six, seven, eight, nine... and then, with my other hand touching each finger, I counted out five hours. It was the most sleep I had had in days. I had been lying in bed with my eyes wide open for about five minutes. Staring at the ceiling fan above me I wondered, *what day is this?* One after another, the days were blending into each other.

Questioning myself, was it yesterday Robin had come over? She's my sister Joyce's daughter, and she had so desperately wanted to help her Aunt Val. I vaguely remember her telling me about a car wash to raise funds for medical bills. The frown line above my eyebrows was feeling like a crease. I reached up to touch it and stroked my forehead. I swirled my finger fast, like an eraser. Everything was so blurry. I couldn't concentrate. *Was that two days ago? Am I losing it?*

Throwing off the cover, I sat up and looked around the room. We really had it looking so pretty; for what? Straightening out my old house dress that had bunched up underneath me, I got up, and after I went to the bathroom and splashed some water on my face, I headed downstairs. Jake must have needed a few more winks and remained in the bedroom.

In the kitchen I caught a glimpse of a note that was perched next to the coffee pot. I recognized Billy's scrawl. He wrote, "Mom, I'll have my cell phone with me if you need me. See you later, Billy." I noticed he had written on the back of an envelope and after turning it over, realized I had to save it; there was a bill inside. I ran the water and placed the coffee filter in the holder. From the window over the kitchen sink, it looked fairly pleasant outside. As soon as I finished preparing the coffee, I headed to the porch. It definitely was going to be another gorgeous day in Florida.

Everything seemed so still until I heard the neighbor's sliding glass door open. I looked over and saw Ann Marie. She must have been waiting for some sign of life at my house. Walking out onto her deck, she yelled over, "Val? Are you gonna be home for a little while?"

Her voice was clear and easy to hear and I answered back, "Yes." My voice was a bit groggy sounding as I hadn't spoken yet, and after clearing my throat, I attempted again, "Yes."

She said, "Good. I have something for you and want to bring it over." Since I hadn't even had my first cup of coffee, I decided to just give her a thumb's up and although not deliberately, mustered up a rather feeble smile.

Seeing my gesture she said, "Okay, see you in a few."

I heard the beep, beep sound the coffee maker makes when it's finished perking. I got up to get myself a cup and carried it out to the table. The coffee tasted delicious and I said, "Mm," out loud. I had a little time to catch up on some things during the morning hours and thought, *I need to e-mail the radio station and see if I can recruit some help.* 'Rise-Up,' the Christian radio show I'd listened to for a number of years

– that's where I originally heard that descriptive phrase, 'prayer warrior' – often aired listeners' prayer requests.

I had just sat down when the doorbell rang. "Coming," I yelled. My old body was not moving around very fast, and as I approached the front hallway, Jake came hustling down the stairs full speed, barking like a maniac. He couldn't quite stop short, and he obviously didn't want to run me over, so he swerved and slid to a stop halfway across the wooden floor. I scolded, "Jake, I have hot coffee!" With scrambling paws he raced me to the front door. The two of us greeted Ann Marie, and Jake welcomed her in traditional Labrador retriever fashion: 'Licky Lab,' and 'Wiggle Butt' affection.

"Oh, Jake, calm down you old oaf!" Anne Marie said in her husky voice. She had long blond curly hair, a quick wit and an infectious sense of humor, but mainly her voice reminded me of the actress, Kathleen Turner. Anne Marie was about thirty-two and could have been one of my children. Her kids were about the same age as my grandkids. We were friends, and the age difference didn't really seem to matter. It felt so good to have her over.

Holding up my coffee I asked, "Would you like a cup?" We walked toward the kitchen.

"Sure. So, what's going on Val? How's Bill? I haven't heard and didn't want to bother you and your family, but figured..."

"What's this?" She was placing a very large pan on the counter. I could see it was hot and peeked inside, the escaping aroma delicious. I hadn't even noticed that she had carried the pan in, what with all of Jakes commotion at the front door.

"Oh, I made a little casserole for you and whoever. It's kind of a beef-a-roni, but I made it from scratch."

"My God, there's so much," I said, heading to the refrigerator. I made some room for the casserole and retrieved the carton of milk.

She rolled her eyes and said, "Please...you'll eat it. My kids love it. You won't have to cook for a couple days if there are leftovers!" I gave her the milk and sugar and watched as she added the ingredients, making her own perfect cup of coffee.

"Still, you didn't have too...but thank you so much. Let's go outside and enjoy this beautiful morning."

Jake followed us outside. Anne Marie spoke to him like he was a person. He was enjoying her attention, and as she scratched his ear, she commented, "Did I tell you how he was crying, Val? Really crying when you all got in the ambulance? Oh, you poor baby. You didn't know what to think. He was pacing around the house like a crazy man. Oh, yes, you remember, don't you?"

"Come here, Jake," I needed to pet his head since I hadn't known about that.

While the two of us sipped our coffee, I filled her in about the last few days, condensing as many details as possible. I just couldn't go into it all again.

She asked, "Are you going down to the hospital today?"

"Of course, but I insisted that the kids return to work today and..."

"Do you want me to drive you?"

"Thanks, but it's all worked out. I think. I'm riding down there with my sister, Joyce. She'll stay awhile. Then later, Shaye will be coming down to visit her dad and will bring me home."

I could feel the tension building inside me as I realized how dependent I was becoming on everyone. Anne Marie sensed something and tried to change the subject. "How did the car wash go? Your niece is such a firecracker. I pulled up to get the car washed and she tried to recruit me." With a big smile and a chuckle she went on. "She had six adults and about ten kids under twelve working in the parking lot at Mel's Diner. I think some of them were your other nieces and nephews. You're grandkids were telling everybody, 'Grandma wants you to pray for Grandpa.' I got up to refill the coffee as she continued, louder so I could hear her. "Most everyone had seen the signs and just wanted to know what had happened to Bill. They were stuffing money in the can and not even wanting to get their car cleaned."

"You know, it was so funny. I was thinking about that this morning. Robin said it went well. I think there's a can. Wait..."

I walked back in and saw it on the kitchen table. "Holy Mackerel, Anne, look at this!" There was a large coffee can with a label taped to it. It read, 'Help our Grandpa.' "It's over flowing; there must be a few hundred dollars."

"Robin is such a good soul. I'm sure the money will help out."

"Gees, I'm gonna cry. Everybody has been so wonderful; I feel so blessed." I didn't want to be so melancholy, so in the happiest voice I could muster up I asked, "Do you know what yesterday was? Our anniversary."

"Oh, you poor baby."

"Yeah, I know. Thirty-seven years."

"God, how old were you when you got married, ten?"

"Thanks. No, eighteen. But right now I feel like one hundred and eighteen."

"Tell me: how can two people be married that long and still be so much in love?"

I thought for a couple seconds, tapping my finger on my temple to make sure it appeared I was really trying to come up with a good answer. I giggled, "Sleep naked!" She let out a laugh, and I couldn't help but join in with her. Girly chit-chat should be a prescription drug. I began to relax for the first time and it felt so good.

"Anne Marie, let me explain. We got engaged in February of 1968, and we planned to marry the following January. By then Bill would have completed his nine month cruise to Vietnam. My parents shared our news with everyone. Announcements were placed in the newspapers both in New York and Florida, shouting to the world that we were engaged."

"We wrote to each other every day sending our love and sharing all our dreams and expectations. The letters were like love songs, and boy did we sing. I couldn't share even half of them with my mom." One of Anne Marie's eyebrows lifted with that remark, and I knew my face was getting pink. Anne Marie and I started to chuckle, and her laugh was so contagious I thought we wouldn't stop.

Trying to gain control, she placed her elbows on the table and held her head in her hands. Looking at me inquisitively she said, "Go on."

"Then one day in March, Bill wrote and said he had been to a meeting with his Navy counselor. The counselor said if we were to marry before his next cruise, he could earn an extra $200 a month just for having a wife. We could save almost two thousand dollars while he was away. Back then, two grand was big bucks. We could have money enough for a down payment on a house when Bill got out of the Navy. I mentioned this to my mom, and the next letter I wrote to Bill was, How about May 11th?"

His letter back to me, said 'I'll be there.'

She spoke with a bit more concern. "Weren't you still in high school?"

"Uh-huh. The wedding was a month before my high school graduation. I practiced writing Mrs. William C. Faulkner, Jr. on all my notebooks and papers. I was so excited. Bill would have to return to his ship on May 22[nd.] We would only have a short time together. Then I would finish high school, find a job, and stay with my mom and dad until Bill returned. I was the happiest woman on earth. It was so hard to concentrate on school, but I knew I had to graduate."

"You didn't think you were too young?"

"Shoot, I couldn't wait. My mom probably figured getting married was better than not, at that point."

We both laughed again so hard, and Anne Marie said, "Where did you go for your honeymoon?"

"West Hampton Beach!"

"Oh, wow, big time!"

I snickered, "Well, it was off season, and what can I say? Cheap! Well, not cheap; you know, lower rates. Okay, back to the good stuff." Chuckling, "We arrived at the hotel late at night. When we entered the lobby we were surprised to see there was a party going on in the lounge. We were greeted by the manager and invited over for a drink. A group of well dressed people, some appearing a little tipsy, were standing at the bar. The manager told us they were celebrating a pre-summer season party. We mingled for a short time and talked with some of the guests. Most everyone guessed that we were newlyweds. I had on a new dress and Bill was still in his uniform. I think the corsage I had pinned to my lapel must have given it away."

"The manager and his wife surprised us with an unexpected wedding present: the owner's apartment instead of the regular hotel room we had reserved. He said the hotel wouldn't officially be open until Memorial Day. No one else would be there during our stay except for an occasional visit from him. The apartment had a small kitchen, sitting room and one bedroom and bath. It was wonderful, much more than we could have ever imagined. The apartment windows faced the Atlantic Ocean. We could hear the surf's cadence as it drummed upon the shore. I thought it was so romantic."

"Red-faced, we made our excuses to the partiers, and with some jeers and knowing glances, we retired to our honeymoon suite."

"I'd brought this beautiful shear white negligee covered with satin and lace. Anxiously, I put it on. My hair was still done up in ringlets that cascaded down over my shoulders, and as I primped, I pirouetted in front of the bathroom mirror and...well, anyway, I looked so pretty, if I do say so myself. When Bill first saw me, he devoured me with his eyes. He had been sitting and waiting with pillows propped up behind him. He had already turned the bed down and had a towel wrapped just below his waist. He stood up from the bed and with such gentle persuasion, took my hand and led me toward... damn! I miss him so much!" I stopped for a breath and then continued. "We got into bed and Bill turned down the lights. Any nervousness was fading away, and it felt so right to lay down with my new husband. Removing my nightie was so; uh... naughty, but then he threw it across the room!"

"What?"

"You heard me." I started to laugh. "I almost died! I screeched, *'why did you do that?'* Bill then told me from this day forward we will sleep in the nude. 'That way', Bill said, 'we could never go to bed mad at each other.' After all, naked people can't be in the same bed, bodies touching, and...well, you know. Seriously, Anne, it's true." I smiled, remembering that moment and told her, "That's why you should sleep naked!" We just grinned, having loved the time together, woman to woman.

"Val, that's a beautiful story. Oh, my God. I'd be satisfied with half your happiness and memories. You two have danced the dance. I just know Bill will be okay. I just know it!"

Chapter 9

Joyce picked me up right on time, and we made it to the hospital by about 12:30 in the afternoon. I had trouble getting my direction at first, but even though she took a different route to Clearwater, I familiarized myself with all the travel possibilities. During the trip she filled me in on how the rest of the family was doing, and I told her of the pleasant morning I'd had with Anne Marie. I still wanted to learn as much as I could about Bill's situation. I asked her if she would help me understand it a little bit better. I asked her to explain, in plain words, some of the things I hadn't yet digested. She was already putting on her imaginary nurse's cap and attempted to answer my questions.

I held her hand as we entered the Intensive Care Unit and guided her to Bill's room. As we entered the room, she allowed her previous education and on-the-job experience to get right to work. I had already been giving her a daily rundown, but today even I could see Bill seemed worse than he had been. His chest was straining for air and crackling noises accompanied each breath. He was looking very pale when, before I could ask Joyce anything, a nurse entered. She held a long suction tube with a bulb on the end and asked if we would step aside. She proceeded to unhook a part of his breathing tube and placed the long stem of the bulb into it. Horrible squishing noises and a gagging attempt from Bill followed. His lifeless body wretched in an upward movement as though he was choking, then fell back to his lifeless position. She removed the tube and discarded brownish, bloody phlegm. I felt a bit woozy and yet stayed to watch as she continued the procedure one more time. The nurse informed us the pneumonia was getting worse. They had started another type of antibiotic to try to see if it could better fight the infection.

Joyce, speaking in medical terms, showed the nurse that she was capable of understanding the technical language better than I. While they talked in their unfamiliar jargon, I stroked Bill's arm and tried to tell him I was there for him. Then, interrupting their conversation, I asked, "Is Bill contagious?" I was concerned about the kids and now Joyce, having been exposed.

The nurse replied, "He really isn't contagious. More than likely, this was caused by a minor abrasion to his throat which occurred when the EMTs were treating him." I didn't have any trouble grasping what she was saying, remembering Bill's original struggle with the paramedics. She continued, "It wouldn't take much to cause an infection, especially in his condition. However, you should use common sense about protecting his environment and limit some visitations…"

"Oh, this is my sister, and other than my kids and I…"

"I meant the smaller kids." I knew she was referring to my grandchildren. "They should wear a mask; children tend to have more opportunities to catch a bug and might not even know it."

"Oh, okay." Joyce and I watched her walk to the desk just outside the room. As she jotted details in the chart book, I searched my sister's face for the slightest facial expression that would signal that this truly was okay. Joyce's mouth appeared tight lipped and seemed to be in a perfectly straight line while her eyes tried to hold back all signs that I might misconstrue. She almost looked guilty, guilty of her own feelings. She deliberately changed over to being a nurse again and explained what some of the machines were doing and why. Although I wasn't grasping it all, I did have a better idea of the what's and why for's when she finished.

Unfortunately, I also read between the lines and could see she was camouflaging her true self to me. She was my sister and that part she had difficulty with. I knew her too well. She glanced at the wall with all the pictures and cards and looked me right in the eyes.

"That's really nice, Val."

"Thank you. One of the doctors said I took away the 'number factor' on Bill's detail sheet. You know, made him a person." I rubbed Bill's arm and kept trying to place his fingers around mine so he would be able to hold my hand. She and I sat across from each other and spoke softly over Bill's body. Joyce continued to stare up at the images his body vibes transcribed to the machines. The blood pressure machine fluctuated every few seconds, and she explained to me what it was doing. Periodically, the cuff on Bill's arm would automatically inflate. Slowly, it would punch out numbers on the screen like a television. Finally, it would stop with a hissing sound. The cycle repeated itself about every ten minutes, capturing its information inside the computer. Physicians could then acquire as much information as they needed and from any pinpointed time of day. Bill's blood pressure would go up and down right before our eyes, but the nurses were attempting to keep it steady and close to 120/70 by regulating meds. Everyone agreed that blood pressure was a really important factor in Bill's life now. I supposed if it went up, it could put pressure on the coil that was inside his brain. I really didn't want to think about that. We chatted for awhile longer, and then Joyce told me she really had to get back.

"Will you be okay?"

"Yeah, of course, I'll just hang out with my honey." I gave her a hug. "I'll walk you down. I need to get something to drink and get some fresh air anyway." Passing the other rooms, I spoke softly, "Shaye's coming later. I'll have plenty of time up here." We left the unit and entered the elevator. Pushing the star button, the doors shut, and we both got that little thrill you get when you're descending. "Egad, I hate that."

"Me too, this one isn't too bad though. I'll sit with you for a few minutes, and then I'll get going."

"All right, I'll have to see if my favorite spot is available." I told Joyce about the table I had commandeered in the corner of the patio and sat down. "Seems it's always empty when I get here. Come, sit down."

Joyce still seemed to be holding back something. Then she spoke in the kindest voice, "Val, I know this all has been so... hard to grasp. Sometimes we have to think about the possibilities..."

I knew where she was going to go with this statement. Instinctively, I figured she had been chosen by the other family members to try to help me through the worst case scenarios; an attempt to prepare me. I imagined how hard this was on her, and in my silence I knew I had to help her out. She continued, "I know nobody likes to think..." She couldn't seem to get it out.

"Joyce, I know this is serious. I realize Bill could die. Joyce, no one can prepare for death. He is alive, and for some reason I truly believe God wouldn't have let him live this long...I believe God will at least let us say goodbye."

"Val, I just was trying to..."

"I know, thank you. But I can't help but think...if I wasn't going to at least get to say goodbye, God would have taken him when this all started. I truly believe this...I'm hoping for more, but I'll take a goodbye. It's God's will. I must, and I will, honor God's will."

With teary eyes she sighed, "I wish I had your faith. I have faith, but..."

"Joyce, I don't want to be alone. I want Bill to be with me for another hundred years. I've already wondered how I could stand it if he left me now."

He and I talked about this sometimes. Both of us would get all teary-eyed even trying to imagine life without the other. The only way that could be is if one of us died.

"Remember Redington Shores and the Bath Club?"

"Yes, the Tides. We used to go swimming there all the time. It was where Grandma used to bring us in '62."

"That's right. Well, Bill and I always said that if something ever happened we could meet there." This was something I never told anyone. It was Bill's and my personal promise to each other. Seems every time we drove down by the beaches, or thought about any of this, we would remind one another of our promise.

"If a time came when we were separated, and if only left to our spirit, the other should go to the beach behind or around the Tides. We would share one last sunset and say goodbye. I'll go there if I need to. For now I'll have to leave it all in God's hands. His will be done."

We hugged each other and I told her, "Drive carefully. I love you."

"Love you too. Talk at you later, bye."

***

Miracles happen in people's lives and I have to admit, sometimes we are too busy to notice them. When I say busy, we could be working or playing, stressing or relaxing. It seems that whenever we're busy, time is passing us by, and we miss the moments that are continually making up our days which become weeks, then months. I personally was so wrapped up with concern and worry over Bill that I hadn't had the wisdom, or a moment, to notice a very visible sign that was there, possibly all of the time.

Arriving back at the unit, I washed my hands in the little sink that was just to the left of his bed then sat down in the chair next to Bill. "It's just me. I'm back, honey." I noticed Bill's skin was feeling dry and gently kissed his arm and his hand. I folded my hands round his right hand and squeezed three times. "I love you, Bill." I silently prayed that God be with us. Speaking to him out loud, I told Bill that I had told Joyce about Redington Shores. I continued to speak even though Bill showed no evidence of coherency. Then, glancing up to the blood pressure monitor, it fluctuated right before my eyes. Going up...up...the numbers held steady at 168 over 90. At first, it scared me as I knew his pressure shouldn't be elevating. So I stopped holding his hand and quietly sat, contemplating if I should call a nurse. It slowly decreased and went back to where it had been.

"Thank you, honey. You were scaring me. I was just watching the monitor and...Bill, it's doing it again. When I speak to you...are you okay? Can you hear me? Oh, gracious God, I think you can hear me."

I went to get the nurse and told her what happened. At first she wasn't sold on this insane idea. "Watch," I said. By now his pressure had returned to a normal level and I began to speak. "Bill, I have just brought a nurse to come see your numbers, and well, she's watching with me. See, they're going up!" The nurse wasn't exactly convinced as she looked and listened to the machine's beeps. Yet her expression certainly led me to believe that this was not an ordinary happening.

"He can hear me! Thank you, Lord, thank you!" The nurse couldn't explain, just remarked, "Please don't do anything to make his pressure go up. He needs to be calm."

I whispered, "Okay." She left me alone and I stared at Bill. My mind, baffled, screamed, *"He heard me! I know it!"*

Our youngest daughter, Shaye, came to retrieve me at about seven P.M. I was ready to leave my post and allow myself some down time. I appreciated her driving over an hour to the hospital after working all day. We walked together down the long halls of the hospital to the parking lot. I had showed her how the pressure went up, and she agreed that her dad could hear me. We went over it again and again as we rode home. Shaye, after a busy day, was still wound up and wanted to talk as well as hear about everything that had happened at the hospital and anything that would give her a little peace of mind about her dad.

Of all my children, Shaye is definitely the one who shares her faith and beliefs with me. We feel blessed with this very spiritual connection. As in the past our conversation led to the promise our Lord has given us: that with hope, love, keeping faith, and believing He would always be there for us, whatever our problems might be. We had living proof so many times. Shaye herself was a walking testimonial.

She had married early like me, but the road she took was not so perfect. She and her first husband were married for about three years, had two children, and ended in divorce. Shaye was hardly twenty-two and on her own. She had to work and nurture the babies solo. Life was hard for her and lonely. Many times she didn't think she would be able to continue life like this. After a few years of going it alone, she was determined for a change. We talked and prayed together often, always hoping for a fresh start with a good man, someone who loved her that she could share life with, someone with whom she could grow old.

Vividly, I recall her saying she was also to blame for her first marriage going sour. Shaye felt that in order to find a great man, she in turn would have to be a great woman.

Shaye made a list of qualities she expected in a great man. The list went on and on. For months it seemed she kept adding just one more characteristic to this perfect man who would become her future husband. He wouldn't drink or smoke or swear; he'd love her children like his own. He would work hard to take care of them. He had to be a Christian and walk a straight and narrow line. He would have to be as gentle as he was powerful, and of course, he would have to kiss really, really, good.

So many times we joked and laughed about this "perfect" man. I'm sure Shaye could have kept adding to her list for years, but she needed someone soon. She prayed daily for her plan to become God's plan also. I prayed for my little girl to find happiness.

God certainly heard our prayers! Brian really is the perfect man for her, and a man I'm proud to call son. They met one day at a grocery store and the rest is history. Shaye and Brian had just celebrated their first wedding anniversary and were on a perpetual honeymoon.

I felt humbled taking her away from her family and having to depend on her this way. I also felt such pride, knowing this young woman with a heart of gold was my child – a mixture of me and her dad – and quite a wonder.

Shaye could see how tired I was and asked if I had stopped to eat during the long day. Lucky me! When I'm involved in something, I forget to eat. I had been running all day on a couple cups of coffee. Shaye wanted to take me out to dinner.

Brian was visiting friends and her two children were staying with Shaye's ex-husband, Chris. She suggested Bob Evan's Restaurant. I agreed but told her I was in no mood to talk to any of Bill's and my friends who worked there. It was a kind of a home away from home for Bill and me. The food was pretty good and reasonably priced. After working all day we found ourselves comforted by familiar surroundings and the pleasant people who work there. It always felt easier to be waited on, and I didn't have to clean up afterwards.

Shaye promised me she would do all the talking if we were bombarded with questions about Bill's condition. When we reached the restaurant, no one was coming in or leaving. In the empty lobby we waited a few minutes for someone to seat us. The unattended cashier's desk, the snack bar, the cooks, had they all disappeared? Finally, Marie walked up to us, surprised to see two new diners. Politely, she gathered some place settings and led us to a table. I recall thinking she didn't seem to be her friendly self. Marie just greeted us as two women and never even acknowledged me. Bill and I had been on a first name basis with Marie for years. But tonight I felt I was dressed in camouflage without Bill, and as weird as it seemed, I found that I actually preferred to be anonymous.

By now it was after eight, and the dinner rush was over. Only a few patrons were seated at tables. I silently thanked the Lord for having Marie guide us to a back, corner table where we could sit, and I could only see the wall. In the past I always hated looking at the wall. On this night, however, I rejoiced having this very special seat. I could eat my dinner and not have to contend with any outside distractions. I could enjoy these moments with my daughter. I was amazed at how beautiful she looked. Although she showed concern for me, it was obvious she was glowing inside and out. Her new life with Brian was her personal miracle and her happiness was apparent.

While we waited to place our orders, Shaye told me that she and her husband wanted to help her father and me with a monetary gift. She's such a sweetheart. As I said no, she insisted, and of course, I became rather emotional for the love and concern she had shown.

I recognized the waiter who came to our table, but he had never served me before tonight. He handed me a menu and one to Shaye. He held a third one in his hands, asking, "Wasn't there a man with you also?"

We looked at each other, saying nothing. The waiter,

puzzled, said. "Oh, I thought I saw another person with the two of you." I assumed he thought Bill had been there with us. Shaye thought differently and excitedly said, "Mom, do you see? The Lord's been here by your side the whole time. You know, He gave you so many signs today…"

I stared at her, silence interrupting her comment. It was true. My brain slowly sorted out what was happening. I was sensing a feeling, up-lifted and energized. I was satiated with such an extraordinary high. Oh, yes…we both felt the glory of the Holy Spirit surrounding us and comforting us that night in Bob Evans.

Cloaked in an amazing grace, we held hands and thanked our Father for His strength and for the hope, courage, love and faith He'd given us. What a blessed Father who cares for his children this way.

God is good. God is great.

We ate our dinner feeling the presence of our Lord and Savior. What an extraordinary moment in time; our hearts glorified as we smiled and shared some gentle laughter rejoicing in this miracle. Jesus promised, "Where two or more are gathered in His name, He would be there also."

Chapter 10

At eight Billy got his crew started from the back porch. The men were preparing to go on an emergency service call that had come in during the early morning hours. Billy owned and operated his own electrical contracting business, and his men were capable of doing the extra work that had to be done. He had offered to temporarily run the two companies; in turn, I would keep the paper portions of the businesses as organized as possible. He knew I needed to have some income until his father could return to work. Although that concept was contrary to popular belief, at least it was the beginning of a plan for the future. I had a slew of personal and business bills to pay and mail to send out, as well as payroll and bank deposits. The agenda would take more time than I had. I wanted to head to the hospital by eleven. Stacie offered to help me get caught up on the week's worth of office work and came to the rescue by nine o'clock. She and I tackled the list with a vengeance.

I carried the stack of unopened mail outside and set it down. It fell over, covering the table top. Shuffling it back into a stack, Stacie, who was already one step ahead of me, said, "Mom, we need a waste paper basket, a stapler, and stamps." I hurried to the office and also returned with a pen and both checkbooks. She sat across from me and assisted in weeding through the important stuff versus the junk mail. "I'll get them set up and you write the checks."

"All right, that will work. Let's start with the personal bills first."

I was reminded of an assembly line as she tore open envelopes, discarding the little paper ads inside, and calling out to me, "Sears: minimum due is $100.00. Account number 5437234351." After writing the check, I tore it out and placed it in the envelope. As I licked the envelope closed, I wondered if we should have bought that new washer and dryer. It was interest-free for a year, but where was I going to come up with the money now, even for the minimum payments? I began a new pile for outgoing mail, and after placing the return address label in the upper left corner and sticking on a stamp, she pushed the stack just little further to the side of the table. Next came Bright House, Progress Energy and, after that, Victoria's Secret. I squirmed in my seat wondering why I hadn't been somewhat more cautious with my spending habits. Our bills were always rather private, and it felt just a little embarrassing having Stacie see where all our money was going. She didn't show the slightest bit of censure, just kept me motivated to finish. Seeing the growing heap of outgoing mail, I was sure I had used up all of our funds.

"That's it, Mom, unless you have anymore inside?"

I swiped my hands together twice, "No. I brought them all out. We're done."

"Okay, I'll run these out to the mailbox."

"Thanks honey." I finished calculating my checkbook register and was happy to see it wasn't in the red, at least not yet. I was amazed at how quickly we had finished and thought how great it was to have her help. Stacie wasn't just a little kid anymore, and I needed to remember that. God knew what he was doing when He gave her to us. Our first, she taught us how to become grownups. Judging by the way she turned out, Bill and I should have earned at least a couple 'at-a-boys'. She was always mature for her age and very smart, too. Having started college at sixteen, she was teaching middle school at twenty. She wouldn't allow me to sit in on her class at school, even when they had those parents' days. I was informed that they were meant for *students*. I teased back, "But I'm a *par-*

ent." When Stacie shared the stories about her teaching experiences, she astonished me with her special gift: the ability to teach.

"Mom, did you know the flag on the mailbox is very loose? I tried to tighten up the screw, but I doubt it's going to hold."

"Oh, Dad said he was gonna fix it... shoot. I'll get it later."

"I e-mailed 'Rise-Up' about Dad and asked them for prayers." Stacie had never been as bold as I when it came to affirming her faith. I couldn't help but smile as I looked at her. I could see that she wanted to tell me what she had done but not necessarily have me make a big fuss over it.

I couldn't help myself. I did make a fuss. "That's terrific! That's great, honey. Thank you! I did, too. Hopefully John Ritter will recruit the 'warriors' for help." She knew she had pleased me, and her crooked little smile made me so proud to have her for a daughter. She was a woman, and I couldn't help but wonder where all the years had gone. I had barely blinked my eyes, and she had gone from five to thirty-five. Had I missed out on anything?

Life wasn't always easy raising one, two, three kids. Early on, we tried to give them all a balance of family life and ethics, but I remember when we lagged on bill paying to feed ourselves. Mortgage payments were late because clothes had grown small. Balancing on the edge of disaster was often a monthly routine.

That brought to mind, "I just thought about something we haven't done in a long time. We'll have to have a Sunny-Side-Up Day, when our lives get back to normal. Well, when Dad comes home."

Stacie grinned, surely remembering how much fun they were. "Yeah..."

"God, I remember the time you wrapped up the picture frame."

She kept smiling and slightly tilted her head, reminiscing with me. When life had been the cruelest and Bill and I had been holding tight to every cent for dear life, the whole family felt the pinched pocket book. Years ago we had come up with a day – not like birthdays or Christmas – just a special day that we named 'Sunny-Side-Up Day.' I gathered change from the junk drawers and unused ashtrays and even the night-stands next to our bed. The total of the found coins came to three, maybe four dollars, and since this was found money, it only seemed appropriate to have a celebration. It's really amazing what one can purchase with so little. Hair ribbons for Shaye, a Pez dispenser for Stacie, a ball for Billy; maybe a coloring book and crayons and some little candies. But it wasn't the gifts as much as the anticipation and pleasant sur-prise of just having a day to be happy. Whenever we were at our lowest, one of the kids might also sponsor a 'Sunny-Side-Up Day,' bringing the promise of better times ahead and cheer back to our life.

"Well, we wanted to give you the frame to surprise you and Dad, and well, a 'Sunny-Side-Up Day,' was just a good excuse to tell the news."

"Believe me; I remember it like it was yesterday. You definitely surprised us!"

"If only you could have seen the look on your faces – all of you! I remember spending just a little bit more money than usual. But there was Billy – and then Shaye – I think they had a couple of friends over. They all loved their little packages tied up in newspaper and bows. But when you and Dad opened up yours and saw the frame…I thought, come on, get the hidden message!"

She had wrapped a photo frame, not a typical frame, but a frame with a stork holding a baby in a blanket molded to the front. Where the picture would be a note saying 'Coming Soon' was inserted. Bill and I stared at that frame for at least thirty seconds; it just wasn't registering in our brains. When it all clicked, I literally jumped out of my seat; our baby was having a baby. We'd be grandparents!

God was good to Bill and me. We were blessed with five grandchildren within a period of less than five years: Katherine, Margaret, Abigail, Kyle, and Lily. Kyle, being the only boy was, of course, our 'favorite grandson,' something we joked about often. I was so glad Bill had had the chance to be a grandpa.

I stood up from the table and walked around to the other side to give Stacie a hug. As I embraced Stacie I whispered, "Thanks for helping this morning. Thanks for Katie, and Maggie, too."

***

We all regrouped by late morning, and with chores completed, the three of us made it to the hospital by one o'clock. Again we had to wait for Bill. We'd been waiting in the ICU family waiting room for about half an hour when Dr. Grady found us. Wearing his suit again, he looked so ceremonial. I was beginning to think his suit was possibly more like armor; wearing it he could maintain and contain his own emotional posture. Today, I perceived a chink in his 'metal suit'. He began, "Mrs. Faulkner, the tests are showing your husband's aneurysm is not leaking. He's well passed the initial forty-eight hours, which is good, but we still can't remove the medications that keep him in a comatose state. We have tried to reduce the levels and he is just not ready. The pneumonia is becoming a problem, and if he doesn't improve, he may have to have a tracheotomy to ensure air gets to his lungs."

I was bewildered, not exactly sure what one had to do with the other. For the good part of a week, I had been waiting for them to bring him out of the coma; it logically seemed I should start there. "Please, no. Please, can't you try...I have noticed the blood pressure machine; he knows when I'm there. How about if I speak to him, and..."

"Mrs. Faulkner, I actually heard about that from the attending nurses, and when the time comes, we may have you speak to your husband. It's already too late this afternoon and the weekend is approaching, so I am just preparing you for what may happen by Monday. Get some rest. You look tired."

Seemed we were going to be at a standstill again. My disappointment was obvious, my optimism fragile. All of us were in the room with Bill while the nurses continued to do their jobs, not one commenting that there should only be two visitors at a time. I watched Bill, his struggle for breaths, his fatigued body. Did he have the strength to fight so hard for much longer? Deep down in my soul I wondered, had God heard me? Bill was my best friend. My mind screamed, *"GOD, HELP HIM!"*

I knew Stacie couldn't stay too long that day. Even though she whispered, I jumped. "Mom, I'm going to have to go now. If you need anything call me, or I'll call you later."

My inner light was dimming but I stood up to hug her.

"All right, give the kids a hug for me. Drive carefully. Thanks again for the help this morning, I really appreciated it. I'm going to stay here with Dad a little longer."

Billy piped up in a slightly louder whisper, "Mom, I'll walk Stacie down."

"Okay."

I could feel the tears rolling down my cheeks as they quietly left the room. I stared at Bill. "I don't know how we got here, kiddo, but I need you to hold on with all your might. I need you to fight. I love you, Bill. I really, really need you."

His drugs must have had him really knocked out; not even the blood pressure machine responded. The room was feeling cold. I adjusted the sheet to cover his bare arms. His hospital gown was loose at the neck and his chest hairs looked like they were pulling from the small round disks that were attached to his chest.

"You look like you are wired for sound. I can't do anything to change that – the monitors are stuck on you with some really sticky stuff. I hope they don't hurt?"

My sobs, nor all the fussing in the world could drown out the tedious hum of the machines. Bill's chest struggled to take each breath. His head was somewhat raised and his feet hung over the foot of the bed.

"That's what you get for being so doggone tall and handsome. Maybe the nurses will scoot you up a little."

I found myself babbling to Bill, yet all the while he laid there, the same as when I had walked in; the same as yesterday. Like all the days before.

In need of a break, I kissed Bill's cheek and told him, "Honey, I'm going to go find Billy. Maybe I'll get something to eat and then I'll come back promise. See you in a little bit, Bill." Only my imagination could hear the response he might have given. I started to walk out and turned for one more look. "Bye, honey."

My lonesome self walked to the end of the corridor where the gigantic double doors automatically opened. I rode down in the huge elevator solo and followed the linoleum path to the outside. I felt like I was dwindling away. I located Billy and signaled to him. He was talking on his cell phone quite a distance down the sidewalk. He acknowledged me with a wave. I sat down, trying to recapture my sanity. Wallowing in self-pity would suffice. Momentarily, I vanished into my own little world, only to be jolted back abruptly when a stranger's voice asked, "You're alone today?"

The little old man stared at me as he waited for a response. I slowly absorbed what he had said. "No. My son is here." I pointed in Billy's direction.

He had a very gentle, kind voice. "How's your husband?"

"He's the same." Answering him, I realized he had probably overheard my family talking the past few days, and even though we hadn't spoke – just nodded to one another – he knew about Bill. "I feel like I know you, but what's your name?"

"Mark."

"Mine's Valerie."

"It's nice to meet you."

"Thank you, you, too. Why are you here? I've seen you since that first day..."

His eyes glistened as his own tears formed little puddles around his beautiful aqua eyes. "My wife, she's up in the Intensive Care Unit. Aneurysm, this is not the first time; she had one a couple years back."

I know my jaw dropped with that statement and struggling to regain composure, stuttered out, "Oh, God, you... you've gone through this two times... twice?"

"Yes ma'am. First time, she came home; she had a few problems. Couldn't quite concentrate, had some trouble with her leg – walking, that is. This time, she's paralyzed down her whole left side." His words were scaring me, and I didn't know how to respond. I could see beyond his wrinkled face that a man with a pleasant appearance once lived. Worry and the difficult times he had obviously been going through made him look an indecisive age; older than what his voice and physical characteristics seemed to portray. "She's going to a nursing home if she leaves here." He corrected himself, "*When* she leaves here."

"I'm sorry. I don't know what to say." Uncomfortably, we halted our conversation. For a few minutes, we just sat in our chairs watching the people come and go. I didn't mind the little chat I was having with Mark but was having a bit of difficulty keeping it going. I decided to try once more.

"My husband is still in a coma. I won't know what he'll be like until…"

I noticed a small figure out of the corner of my eye. I stopped talking to look directly to my left where a little girl stood next to me. She was about two or three years old. In the past, Bill always referred to me as a kid magnet. Wherever we were, a child would smile, wave with two or three of their little fingers as they shyly held their hand up close to their cheekbone, or we would play peek-a-boo by cupping our hands over our faces. I loved children and presumed they must have thought this grown-up was just a big kid, too. The little girl had sandy blond hair pulled back into two short pony tails. Some stray strands that had fallen out of the bands softly curled about her beautiful face. Her pink and white pinafore seemed a bit too large for her small frame, and one shoulder showed where the dress had slipped down. She wore pink flip flops and stared at me with big blue eyes.

"Well, look at you. You look like an angel. Are you a little angel sent here to cheer me up? How old are you?"

"I'm three, or five."

"Oh, I see. I think you look three. What's your name?" She spoke so quietly I couldn't understand. "I'm sorry, what did you say your name is?" This time she didn't say any words but instead walked around to the front of my chair. I commented, "You are just so pretty. I like your dress."

"Thank you."

As she stood there I glanced around to see who she was with. Glancing first at Mark, I asked her, "Where's your mommy?" Mark shrugged his shoulders as though to inform me he didn't see anyone that seemed to match up with her.

She answered "In the hobsbitul."

"Oh…"

"Is that where your mommy is?"

"No. My husband is in the hospital."

"Is he your daddy?"

"She's something else, isn't she?" The voice came from a young man who was suddenly standing next to me. I don't know why, but I started from the bottom and worked my way up to his face. He wore old sneakers, ragged jeans, and an oversized tee shirt with many colors and a band name. His arms were covered with tattoos, but his facial piercings' were a total surprise, as was his hair; it was about four inches long with wide streaks of pink and blue, spiked out in deliberate disarray.

"Uh, yes, I was just enjoying her company and wondered who she was with."

"She's with me. Her mom's inside; they don't know what's wrong with her yet. This little one has been a perfect angel, under the circumstances."

"I was just saying that…" Looking back down at the little girl, I smiled. "You know, little angel, I will say a prayer for your mommy to get all better real soon, okay?"

"Yes." She jumped up from her spot in front of my chair.

I was glad my first superficial impression of the young man hadn't locked any doors. He spoke kindly in agreement, "Oh, we have been praying." He went on to praise God with gracious conviction and beheld the power of prayer dear to his heart. He boldly attested, "I believe in miracles."

What an exceptional man of faith, I thought. Then, reaching out his arms to pick the little girl up, he spoke to her,

"Come on, how about we go see how Mommy's doing?"

She nodded her head affirmatively to him and reached out as if to hold my hand. I reached out to her, and we touched our hands in a friendly spirit of good-bye, but then she bent down and kissed mine. At that moment I felt so pleasantly blessed.

What a sweet child. I brought her hand up to my lips and kissed hers, too.

They disappeared amongst the rest of the wandering souls. I looked back at Mark. "Did you see that, Mark? I think I've been kissed by an angel." He could see my spirits had shifted from our first conversation, and I could see that watching me with the little girl had sparked his own flame of hope. His teary eyes still showed such pain.

"I really never do this… just take my hand."

He reached out. There on the patio I needed to speak in prayer out loud. With our hands held tight, I prayed for Mark's wife. I prayed for Bill and I prayed for the mother of the little girl. That little angel: so small, so Godlike. Have you ever met a child who was less than perfect? She had inspired me. She had to be a sign from our Father; a blessing from above.

Chapter 11

Billy walked up; he finished making his calls. "Are you ready to go back up to the room, Mom?" I dropped my cigarette into the Styrofoam cup of old coffee and carefully placed it in the trash canister at the corner of the patio.

Turning back at Mark, I waved. "Bye, Mark. Talk to you later." Billy was already waiting by the door to go in so I added a little skip to my walk.

As I approached him, Billy asked quietly, "What's that man's name – the one you were talking to?"

"Oh, that's the man who has been out here every day since Monday and I finally met him. His name is Mark. You know I just had the most inspirational moment."

"Why do you think that?"

We walked at a brisker pace through the corridors. I didn't even have to pay attention to the paths as we found our way to the elevator. I started to tell my story about the little angel and told Billy I really felt like God was giving me a sign. "I just feel good...like something good is going to happen. I'm not sure why, I just..."

In a lighthearted way, almost mimicking the way I speak, he replied. "Okay. I'm gonna feel good, too." I felt like swatting him but knew he was just playing around with me. At the fifth floor we made our way down the hall to the great big double doors. He gave the button a pop and the doors slowly swung open. It seemed my attitude was encouraging him to feel slightly giddy, too, but we needed to calm down as we entered the ICU.

"Shh!"

Billy, with a slightly sarcastic voice and a glare at me, whispered. "Okay, Mom."

Coming back to Bill's room, I was definitely feeling a little stronger and walking a little taller. Walking in sync, side by side, Billy and I both took bigger steps. But we weren't going faster, just being silly. *With music and song, Dr. Grady in his metallic suit, we could have been skipping off to see the Wizard.* It was goofy and slightly mischievous, but we kept watch that no one would actually notice us. Arriving at the entry to Bill's room, we were ready to settle down and behave. The restrained mind-set returned.

Perhaps I wasn't completely somber enough; my whisper came out in a kind of sing- song fashion, "Bill, we're back. Billy is here with me." I began where I had left off, telling Billy and Bill about the rest of my story when I stopped short. "Billy, look at the blood pressure machine. It's doing it again when I speak. See if it does that for you."

"Hi, Dad, I'm here with Mom..." his voice wavering, he stopped. The machines didn't show any change. I could see this was uncomfortable for him.

I began again. "Bill, I was just wondering...if you tried real hard to open your eyes, well, you could see us. Want to try? I love you honey. Don't be afraid."

I'm really not sure if I expected any response, but I needed to give it a shot. I prompted Bill a couple more times, and that's when Bill's head turned about two inches to his right. I had a difficult time keeping my composure. My voice was shaky but I spoke as gently as I could.

"Bill, you can do it; open your eyes." Billy and I watched in silent excitement as Bill's eye lids fluttered rapidly.

Like anyone who has had their eyes closed in sleep, he

strained to open his. It was maybe 15 seconds that Bill squinted, leaving his brows drawn tight across his forehead. He persisted and for about the next 30 seconds his beautiful blue eyes were open wide and looking my way. I stared at him in amazement, but instantly, was horrified. I could immediately see that even though his eyes were open his inner soul was not visible. I waited for the slightest glimpse of his personality, but his glazed stare was hollow. His pupils' minute. Any emotional connection was void. My husband, my love, was not present. A surreal space, a transparent wall, separated us from one another.

His unattached gawk sent a chill down my spine. The shiver traveled quickly from my shoulders down my back; the jolt making my body shimmy. I brought one hand to my mouth to silence any gasp. I couldn't look at him this way. My blood was settling in my feet. I buckled into the chair next to the bed. Speechless, quiet, shocked.

Billy came to my side of Bill's bed. He knew I wasn't reacting the way he would have expected me to. From where he stood he hadn't experienced the full impact of what I had just seen. Unsure, his vague expression questioned me as he reached out his hand to help me stand. I stood and hugged my son.

His arms wrapped around me flashed bittersweet memories of his dad. With my face scrunched into his chest, I couldn't hold back the tears. I sobbed as my son embraced me; he held me in silence. I couldn't say what I had seen. I sniffled as a choked up feeling tightened around my throat. Billy must have sensed my need to get out of Bill's room as I pushed away from his arms. I could see the wet areas my tears had made on his tee shirt. Brushing them as though they would disappear like powdery dust, I sniffled, "I'm sorry."

"Don't worry 'bout that. I think we should go home now, Mom. You're tired and Dad needs to rest."

With short breaths all I could sob out was, "Okay... let's go."

As we started to leave, I paused. "Wait..." and retraced the few steps to the edge of the hospital bed. Bill's eyes were closed again, and he had peacefully returned to that place that nobody can remember. I adjusted his sheet, leaning over to gently kiss his cheek. "I love..." My tears were blurring my vision. I turned, grabbing a tissue. After wiping my face I attempted to speak again. "I'll... see you...tomorrow... honey."

Exiting the building I didn't take the time to notice a single person. I just wanted to get away, far, far away. I wanted – needed – time to sort my feelings and space to find the spirit in me that, when I had seen Bill's eyes, had just turned off. Billy didn't say a word, just walked beside me until we were outside. He handed the valet parking attendant the slip of paper needed to retrieve the Jeep.

It felt like a sauna outside compared to the ice cold hospital. We commented about the heat while waiting for the man to bring our car. In a strange way, it almost felt nice to feel the warmth. I needed to ask, "Did you see his eyes?"

Billy nodded, "Yes." As though considering an explanation for me, "Dad's on a lot of drugs. It's got to be the drugs!"

The vehicle was stifling from sitting in the hot sun all day so, before even climbing in; we unzipped the windows and turned up the air conditioning. Billy wanted to drive, but I was already on the driver's side. "I'll drive." I needed to keep my mind busy doing anything other than thinking about Bill's eyes. Traffic was horrendous. Most people on the road had probably just finished work. It was about quarter till five and seemed everyone was trying to get home. The sun was still high in the sky. I decided to take the scenic route that Joyce had driven the day she had brought me to the hospital. Fortunately, Billy was familiar with the way, taking all the guesswork out of the trip. When he could see I was getting a bit confused, he would calmly direct me to the correct street. Road construction and detours I didn't remember from the first trip caused minor delays.

It took us about an hour and forty minutes to drive into Pasco County. Barely a word was spoken until I headed down one more back road to get off US 19.

"Mom, why are you turning here? It's faster on nineteen." Surely his patience was fatigued and the back road would add about ten minutes.

"I'm driving – I want to go this way. I'm just avoiding the traffic wherever I can."

"You know, I have Abbie tonight."

He had told me that earlier but I had forgotten. She would be spending the weekend with us as well. "Uh, I know. We'll be home soon. Don't worry. We'll go home and get cleaned up. All of us are invited to Grandma's for dinner. Aunt Kathie and Uncle Dave are bringing meals on wheels for everyone." I thought longingly about a home cooked meal and presumed Billy was, too. "Sound good?"

"Yeah, it does. What's she making?"

I couldn't help but laugh. "Does it matter? It's not beef-a-roni again. I'm sure whatever she makes will be great."

"Oh, I just thought maybe she told you. I'm cool. Abbie will be happy to see her Great Grandma and Great Grandpa."

"I can't wait to see 'Abadabba.' I could use a huggy-bear or two, and she'll be great for that. Do you have to go pick her up?"

"No. She's getting dropped off about seven."

I glanced at the radio, "Oh, dear. Think we can make it? Want to call her?"

"We're okay, Mom. I already did. You didn't hear me on

the phone?"

I guessed I was concentrating on driving or zoning out to the music. I glanced at his smile and nodded, "Well, that's good. Glad you called her." The drive had done wonders for me. Only a little step forward, but I had taken an opportunity to be in command of myself. So many times in my life I'd let others be in charge of everything, and I really needed to grow up and be ready to handle life's challenges. I had to be able to handle whatever was in store for me and Bill.

Pulling down our street I pushed the remote for the garage door and cocking my head, gloated, "We made it, safe and sound. I can't remember the last time I drove for that long."

"It's like riding a bike…"

"I guess so."

***

Billy, Abbie, and I made it to my parent's house just in time. Kathie and Dave had already set the table with Mom's china dishes and were placing the plates of food on the table.

Kathie peeked out from the kitchen. "Good, you're here. Dave, would you take off the Saran Wrap?"

"Sure, hi, Val, Billy, Abbie, how are you all doing?"

Answering for all of us I spoke out, "We're hanging in; smells absolutely delicious!"

Billy and Abbie agreed. As Kathie brought one more plate of food to the table, she called out, "Come and get it!"

The nine of us sat down in the dining room. The large, dark wood table had plenty of room. The huge colonial hutch still looked beautiful. My parents had brought it from New York when they moved here in 1974. Following their three girls to Florida, they fully retired that year. Early retirement gave them many years of happiness along the shore of Port Richey's Miller Bayou. Mom and Dad sat at the two heads of the table, Joyce and her husband, Mickey, Kathie and her husband, Dave sat along one side. Billy, Abbie, and I sat along the other side. I felt so honored and loved. My Dad looked at us all and folded his hands. The rest of us had already joined hands so he reached out to Billy and Joyce sitting on either side of him. In unison we said grace. And then the questions started. As we served ourselves, Billy and I made an attempt to give everyone an answer for their concerns.

Dad took the floor when he stated, "It just doesn't feel right, you know, Bill not here." His voice silenced as he held back a tear. Mom agreed with him and taking her hanky blotted her eyes. Her expression told me she wished this wasn't happening to Bill and me.

Breaking the momentary silence, someone said, "Kathie's *'Famous Grandma Chicken'* must be good! Everybody's so quiet." A few chuckles and smacking of lips and we all gave our compliments to the chef.

I couldn't eat very much and felt it an opportune time to tell my little angel story. I put a little theatrics into it to hold their attention. I wanted them to capture the moment so they, too, would feel what I'd felt. Quietly they listened, just waiting for every word. By now everyone had finished eating, and I said, "I want to tell you the rest, but before I do I am asking you to pray for Bill. I know I have asked that already, but I'm asking again. I need you to pray for a miracle." I told them about Bill opening his eyes. I had a difficult time telling this part and yet found the strength to say, "That's why I need you to pray for a miracle." I added, "And, please, tell anyone you talk to, to pray as well."

I thanked God for all of them and enjoyed their company for a little longer. When we got home, I helped Billy get Abbie ready for bed. Cherishing all her hugs and kisses, I said,

"Sleep tight! Don't let the bed bugs bite. Love You!"

"I love you, too, Grandma."

I went downstairs to the office. It was 10:47 P M on Friday, May 13, 2005. I pulled up my e-mail.

Chapter 12

At the fireplace

The remainder of the pure white sheet of typing paper was blank. I released the page and watched it float to the tile floor. That shivering tickle reoccurred, making me quiver as it traveled up my spine. I hated the pain that day had brought and hated reliving Bill's blank stare. My back and neck felt stiff. I twisted my body until I heard the crackling noises that relieve stress.

Jake was asleep, his head resting on my lap. Upon awakening he opened his big brown eyes, not moving a muscle. "I have to get up; should we have some lunch?" Jake moved nonchalantly as I groaned. Standing, I stretched my arms, my hands coming close to touching the ceiling. Bringing them back down, I shouted. "God..." I headed to the coffee pot and, stomping my feet one after the other, yelled, "This is insane! What the hell am I doing?"

I fed Jake then stared at the steam spiraling upward from my cup. My head shook in dismay, wondering how I would be able to tell the stories in a way that someone – anyone – might want to hear.

Spoken a lot softer and as more of a question, "God...?" My own mind answered myself matter-of-factly. God knew I wasn't a quitter. I had to – needed – to keep my promise.

Deciding to continue for at least a little while longer, I picked up the whole box of papers from the hearth and placed them on the kitchen table. The sliding folders shifted gradually to one side of the carton, except for the folder with a tab that read E-MAILS. The folder had a yellow post-it-note stuck on the outside. Written in red marker, the note read, 'Don't forget these!'

I picked up the folder and opened it up. About ten pages were stapled together. The first dated May tenth. I didn't have any problem remembering that day. I had e-mailed Bill every night upon returning from the hospital. Writing him had been somewhat of a comfort. Other than when he was in the Navy, we had never been separated.

***

In May 1968 we spent eleven wonderful days together on our honeymoon. With dread we faced the day Bill would have to depart. The Vietnam War had not stopped because we were married, and he had used up his leave. It was time to get back to his job in the United States Navy. We arranged Bill's bags in the trunk and had about three hours until his plane would leave J.F.K. in New York; the ride to the airport would take at least two. Our extended family hugged and kissed us as we left for the city.

Singing along with the music playing on the radio, we would comfort each other with an occasional touch. We talked and tried to keep as 'up' as possible, knowing it would be nine months before we would see or caress one another. His ship would sail out of San Francisco in less than one week and return at the end of January. He would have to get back to Whidbey Island, Washington, before I could join him at the naval base in February of 1969.

As we cherished our last lingering kiss and hugged our last hug, we promised to write each other every day we were apart. We sealed the promise with one more kiss, and with tears rolling down my cheeks, I waved to the plane as it soared into the sky and out of sight.

Beginning that night I kept my promise and wrote the first of hundreds of letters that would follow. Bill did the same, never missing a day. In those letters we told of our days, our separate lives. We would tell all of our dreams and desires for our future together. Finally, if we could hold off until the middle of the second page, we would make love via snail mail. We acted out our kisses and hugs. We told of our emotions, what we would experience if we were together. We discovered every part of our love and celebrated our union thousands of miles apart. Most letters sizzled with intensity, and although the separation was extremely difficult, we held tight to our faith, loyalty and the promises we'd made to one another. Our wedding vows included: 'What God hath brought together, let no one put asunder.'

I went on to graduate from high school and found my first real job. For sixty dollars a week plus room and board, - I was delighted to have landed such wealth. Bill mused with his buddies that he had sent his wife off to camp for the summer.- Hired as a camp counselor for a Catholic children's home located on the north shore of Long Island in a town called Shoreham, I lived in a cottage with eight girls ranging in ages from ten to twelve. Since I wasn't twenty-one, a nun, Sister Diane, stayed in the one and only bedroom the cottage had. The girls and I shared the dormitory and the single bathroom. At first, my Pollyanna upbringing found me in much dispirit as I learned about the hardships these children had suffered. Some came from poor, neglected families, while others were actually victims of abuse. Some girls' parents were convicted *criminals and were spending time in jail. It took weeks for the girls to respond to me and realize that I was not the enemy. I was too old to be their friend, yet too young to gain their respect. Eventually, I won their confidence and felt blessed to know each and every child. They, too, let their hardened surface shells soften enough to learn to trust in another person, something they had all learned to avoid.*

At camp the kids, counselors and administration staff would meet in the media/activities room every day after lunch and before swim time to have mail call. I would wait anxiously for my name to be called. There were days that would pass and my spirits would be saddened that I had not received any mail. I never accepted that the mail system out in the Pacific Ocean wasn't a daily occurrence. Sometimes Bill's letters would be held on the ship for over a week. If the mail plane didn't pick up his mail...well, I couldn't receive any. The same went for him aboard ship. Gradually, Bill and I learned to cope with this and looked forward to ten to fourteen letters delivered at one time. Then the cycle would begin again. He put numbers on the outside of his letters so I could start at the beginning when I opened them.

The whole group would experience my pleasure when finally after days, weeks, the mail lady called out my name. They all applauded with enthusiasm. Retrieving my mail, I'd hold it close to my heart. With a sigh of relief, I hoped I would make it until the next time.

By August I had filled a box with love letters; Bill had as well. We both missed one another terribly. He had begun a short timer's chain to count down the days left at sea. About halfway finished with his tour, he was notified that his Dad was very ill. He would need to take emergency leave and return to the states. Bill spent the next thirty-six hours boarding helicopters, planes, and taxis' to place him back in Florida, U.S.A.

I flew from New York to Florida and met him when he ar-

rived. Mixed feelings groped at the two of us, and we had dif-ficulty rationalizing our happiness with his dad's suffering. His father died at the age of fifty-six.

When you are eighteen and your husband is twenty-two, fifty-six seems far off. Our young lives were bounced back to reality abruptly with little time to consider how precious life is. Bill was sent back to his ship and back to the war. I fin-ished camp, and when the children returned to school, was hired as seasonal help in a local family-owned department store, starting after Labor Day.

Our letters continued, but after being together for the short two weeks, it was harder for the two of us to be sepa-rated again. Days seemed longer and nights broke our hearts. We both dreaded the next few months.

Thanksgiving came and Christmas was just weeks away. I drove to work in chilling snow and sang Christmas songs with the radio. Each morning, like clockwork, the song 'I'll be Home for Christmas' would play. The song had not been fa-miliar to me, but I quickly memorized the lyrics and sang along. I heard it over and over at work, too. The song was played every hour in rotation with other holiday music. By mid-December my silly mind fantasized that Bill would sur-prise me and come home for Christmas. I truly began to be-lieve this, my heart skipping a beat every time I heard the song play.

I would imagine sitting by the window on Christmas Eve, staring out at the fresh fallen snow. A cab pulls to a stop in front of my house. Getting out of the car was a sailor. Could it be? Was it? Bill? There he was in his uniform, standing at the edge of the driveway while flurrying snowflakes silently drifted. Colorful lights dancing in the neighboring windows reflected their twinkle on the fresh new blanket of white. He had his sea bag and a wrapped present. Placing them on the ground as I ran to him (of course in slow motion), he'd hold out his strong arms as I leapt into them. Having been lifted gently, I'd slowly slide down the front of his tall body bring-ing us very close to one another. With my feet barely touching the ground, standing on just the tips of my toes, he would look down at me, his most beautiful blue eyes gazing into mine, pull me close and kiss my yearning lips.

I glanced over the folder of e-mails and briefly re-read the letters I had sent to Bill that week. My heart ached re-membering how scared I was when I wrote them. "Jake, what do you think, should I use these?"

Chapter 13

Tears were blurring my vision as I sat staring at the computer monitor, that evening. It was getting so late. Franticly I typed my nightly message to Bill.

I hit send with the curser. Then decided it wouldn't hurt to e-mail John Ritter from 'Rise-Up' one more time too. I gave a plea for prayers and told him I believed I really, really needed a miracle. By the time I finished and decided to go up to bed, I found Billy fast asleep on the couch. Letting Jake out for his last potty call, I shut off the lights and the TV. I placed a throw blanket over Billy. I wouldn't disturb him to go up to his bed. Poor kid, he didn't stir, and it appeared nothing could awaken him. Running the businesses and taking care of Mom was hard work. Jake tagged alongside me up the steps and followed me to check on Abbie. She was snuggled up under the covers in Stacie's old bed. I smiled as I listened to her gentle breathing and remembered when Bill was building that bed.

* * *

It was for his first princess. Over the years I was always dreaming up new ideas and would ask Bill if he could do it. He would give my requests deep consideration, but it might have been days, weeks or even months before we would actually get the project started. As his own mom would say, "When the spirit moves him..."

When the spirit moved him, he embellished upon my original ideas and created outcomes that would totally amaze me. I never imagined a bed that would be notched into the wall. Looking from the doorway into the room, one could see an arch on the adjacent wall and beyond the arch a nook with a platform large enough to hold a single mattress. Stacie would climb up a step to get into bed and could cozy up in her very special sleeping quarters that her dad had made for her. It was charming, and, over the years, all the grandkids argued over who would get to sleep in the bed in the wall.

***

I kissed Abbie and whispered, "Tonight you have the room all to yourself. Sweet dreams."

Down the hall in our bedroom, Jake circled in his doggy bed until he found just the right spot to lie down. It was after midnight and I debated whether to call the hospital. I was sure I would at some point, just not now. After washing my face and brushing my teeth, I combed my hair. The mirror told me I was looking tired and drawn. Some gray was peeking through my hair. *I'll have to color it soon, or I'm going to start looking my age.* Glancing under the sink I found a box of hair coloring and rested it on the countertop. *Maybe I'll have time tomorrow...it's too late tonight.* I picked up the brush and detangled my hair for a minute longer, making sure it all hung down my back, away from my face. The crinkled waves my braids had made gave it a full and fluffy look. I admired how long it had become. *Bill, you would love my hair tonight.*

Finished in the bathroom, I turned the light on in the bedroom. Jake stretched out his paws and looked at me, surely wondering when I'd settle down. Getting into bed I stretched for the remotes on Bill's nightstand. *The green and white one works the bed...the black one the TV.* After fiddling with them I eventually got the bed in a comfortable position and found Jay Leno.

Good, I did it. Bill was 'King of the Remotes' and I was regretting I hadn't developed that skill. I sat staring at the television, not finding anything entertaining except for the shades of light that were being strewn across the room. My thoughts blanked out the TV; the blah, blah, blah of voices couldn't penetrate my mind. Normally, I would have been snuggled up next to my hubby. I missed him so much. Leaning up on my elbow, I grabbed the extra pillows and patted them down, lining them up on Bill's side of the bed. He had always joked that I allowed him the area of a return address on an envelope, so I made sure I gave my 'Pillow Bill' a modicum of extra space. I needed one more pillow to accommodate his size, and with only minor adjustment, he was perfect.

I wasn't sure how long I could stand the wondering and waiting. *Bill, honey, I promise you whatever it takes; I'm going to be right here for you.*

I woke up with one leg slung over my 'Pillow Bill' and one arm stretched around the middle in a secure hug. I had drifted off with the television on. I groped around the comforter until I found the remote and fortunately found the off button, first try. I resumed my position and sighed. *Good night...* I hadn't given another thought to calling down to the hospital.

***

Saturday morning I arose early and frantically placed my call. I found out Bill was already having some tests but was assured there had been no changes. The nurse on duty was glad I had had a good night's sleep. Agreeing, I hurried to begin my morning ritual. I planted myself out on the porch with a fresh cup of coffee to experience all my little blessings.

I was enjoying the sunshine and the sight of all the pretty little flowers that ran along the fence at the edge of the yard when Abbie, realizing I'd been outside for awhile, asked, "Grandma, can I go for a swim? The pool is nice and warm."

I thought it was rather early but decided I could keep an eye on Abbie while she entertained herself, so I acknowledged her, "Sure. Get your suit on but stay in the shallow end, okay?"

"Thanks, Grandma!"

By ten o'clock the phone was ringing off the hook. Many distant relatives were sending their regards and hoping to hear of improvement. They figured they'd be able to catch me in during the morning hours before I left for the hospital. One after the other, I explained what was happening and asked that they would take part in praying for a miracle. Bill's aunts, uncles, nieces, and nephews were all on board.

I received one more call from my close friend in California. Having known Hal since we were kids, he was like a cousin to me. He had lived out west for probably fifteen years after retiring from the New York City Police Department, but his Brooklyn accent held true.

"Val, how are ya?"

I held back a laugh. I had forgotten how we true 'New Yawkas' spoke. Hearing his voice after so long was wonderful. His new work kept him busy, and it was such a fascinating job: bodyguard to the stars. He wasn't interested in talking about his life, though. Instead, he had deep concern for me and had gotten up extra early to call. I almost felt like agreeing when he offered to fly to Florida to help. I hadn't seen him in ages, and it had probably been a year since we'd spoken on the phone. E-mail had kept us in touch, closing the gap that distance and time creates.

He assured me throughout our conversation that we were in his thoughts and beckoned, "If you need anythin' dear, I'm here."

"Thank you so much. It's been wonderful just hearing your voice." Then I contemplated, "Well, there is one thing…"

"What?"

"Well, if you want to tell everyone you know in California to say a prayer, I'm looking for a miracle, ya know?" He paused momentarily. I assumed this a larger task than what he had anticipated.

Then, speaking up loud and clear, he said, "I'll take the job, done deal, Val."

"Thanks, Hal. I love you."

"Love you, too. Bye."

I hung up the phone and looked up towards heaven and asked God, "I hope you hear all of them?" Rephrasing that; "Please hear us."

Splashes of water brought my attention back to Abbie.

"Grandma, why don't you come for a swim? The water is delightful!"

Abbie had heard me use that description many times. My grandmother always said, 'the water is delightful,' and I had always said that, too, since I was a child. I couldn't help but chuckle as I replied, "I'll have to pass this time. Pretty soon I will need to leave for the hospital. Okay?

"Well, will you watch how long I can hold my breath underwater?"

"Of course, want me to count?"

"Yes. Start when I go under."

She took a deep breath and submerged. I began counting. When I got up to twenty-five, I thought, 'Gees, she's good.' At thirty-eight and one-half she sprung out of the water and actually had enough air left to immediately ask, "How did I do?"

"Great! Almost thirty-nine. I'm impressed."

"Cool! Me too, think that's the best so far; again?"

"Take a rest. I don't want you to get hurt."

"Okay, grandma. Come here, Jake!"

Before I could stop him, Jake jumped into the pool, diving down under the water in search of a sunken pool toy.

"Ah... oh, darn it." I sighed. "Whew... it's too late. He's wet."

Jake loved the water and rarely listened to my instructions when any of the grandchildren were around. He surfaced and swam to the edge of the pool. Sitting down on the step he casually glanced over at me. I knew he wanted me to say it was okay, but instead I just glared at him. He remained still; he hated disappointing me. He looked over every few seconds, now unsure where this was going. I couldn't keep my mad face on forever and began to laugh. I gave in.

"Go ahead, boy. Go swim." Back in the pool for some laps, he indulged Abbie with all his tricks and her laughter was music to my ears.

Overall, it had been a pleasant morning. By early afternoon Abbie had gone back to her mother's house. I was ready to go visit Bill and the kids wanted to go, too. The four of us headed down for the afternoon. The hospital visit was similar to all the other days; by the time we were heading home, I was exhausted and cranky. I knew the week had been a tough one for all of us and felt I should be the first to set the others free. "Please, it's Saturday and the day is thinning. Go, be with your families and don't worry about me."

The girls didn't try to hide the fact that they did need to be with their families. Gradually, they headed out with very little persuasion. Billy needed to pick up Abbie from her mother's. "See ya later, Mom. I won't be long."

I waved him on and told him to drive carefully. It had been awhile since I had had all this attention, and I appreciated them all but couldn't help but sigh with a little bit of relief when I went back to sit at the kitchen table all by myself. The kitchen was showing a week's worth of neglect. I thought about our dreams of selling. I thought about Bill and me eating together, sharing thoughts and conversation. It had been six whole days. Holding my head in my hands, I felt total dismay. *God... I can't stand this... I want my life back... I want Bill back here in our home. I just want life to be normal again!*

Slipping out of my seat, I went to the chair where Bill usually sat. I sat down and imagined I was on his lap, cradling my arms around him. It was as though he had his arms wrapped around me, too. I thought about how I used to sit on his lap and how normal that felt.

We swayed in the chair, rocking gently, soothing away the fears.

Chapter 14

The 'Rise-Up' jingle was music to my ears. I hoped words of inspiration would help me continue this journey I was on. I had been up since about six-thirty. Already I had consumed about five cups of coffee and smoked way too many cigarettes. Apprehension consumed me. The testimonials and country music filled me with the Spirit, and I was able to enjoy the morning God had given me, but I couldn't help but wonder if my e-mails had gone through. Had John read them? Was he bombarded with so many he hadn't had time to read them all? I hoped beyond hope that John Ritter would ask the warriors to say a prayer and impatiently listened to the show waiting for his words.

Billy and Abbie joined me out on the porch at about eight o'clock. For a Sunday this was pretty early for them to be up, but like me, they had placed a lot of their hope in John Ritter's recruitment. During the commercial Billy told us both, "I feel like John Ritter is going to mention Dad, and if he asks for prayers…well, I just know Dad will be okay, Mom. I know it."

"God knows. I hope so! I've been listening since early this morning and nothing yet. I hope he received my e-mails."

"Grandma, why don't you call in to the station?"

"Abbie, honey, I couldn't speak on the phone and not get all upset. I can't. But, if you want to…?"

"No, I can't either." We looked at Billy. He lifted his hand in a motion that undeniably suggested a 'nay' on that option.

"Okay," I said. "How about while the commercials are on we say a prayer together so that John Ritter will tell the warriors about Grandpa." All agreeing, we held hands. We said our own silent prayers, each of us hoping for a miracle.

The next two hours were special. We were together and praising the Lord, something the three of us had never done with each other. In between the calls and testimonials that came over the radio, we cried or laughed or prayed. As the show was coming to an end, we were sitting on the edge of our seats; four hours had passed and John hadn't mentioned Bill. I was saddened but determined to continue listening until the very end of the show. I couldn't give up. As the jingle at the end of the show began, I could see the enormous defeat in Billy's eyes. Abbie, too, appeared laden in disappointment.

Then, out of the radio loud and clear John spoke over the music. "Before I say good-bye, I have a request for prayer. Bill Faulkner of Port Richey has suffered a ruptured brain aneurysm and has been in a coma for this past week. His wife is asking that we help her pray for a miracle. Keep him in your prayers today." And as he ends each and every show he continued, "That's it. Honey, load the kids in the car. Be sure you're all wearing your seat belts, and I'll see you in church." And the 'Rise-Up' tune ended the program.

First, we were stunned. As we clarified in our minds what our ears had just heard, the three of us simultaneously jumped up into a huge hug. We jumped up and down together and danced joyfully. Floating on a cloud and overcome with happiness, the three of us yelled and screeched with enthusiasm. We were filled to the brim with excitement, hope and faith!

For the rest of the morning, the birds sang louder and the flowers smelled sweeter. I waited for Stacie's arrival so the two of us could take our trip to the hospital. Shaye would stay home today and tend to all the things a mother should do on her day off from work. I let her know we would keep her informed. Billy, too, planned a break so he could spend some quality time with Abbie. When I talked to Stacie, she reassured me that she really could take the time away from housework and acted as though this was no inconvenience whatsoever. She definitely wanted to go. Now that we knew several different routes to Clearwater, the routine was actually becoming less of a hassle. Depending, of course, on traffic, the scenic drive along the water's edge was the most pleasant.

***

Stacie and I watched the choppy waves on the inter-coastal waterway as we drove through Dunedin. Riding in her SUV instead of the Jeep, I enjoyed the trip. I had been trying to save her wear and tear on her vehicle, but today she opted for comfort and luxury. The tan leather seats still had that fresh smell of newness, and the car seemed to float.

"This is so quiet and smooth."

"Yes, we love it. Makes driving pleasurable."

"Dad and I didn't get the Jeep for comfort...it's just a hell of a lot of fun! Days like today we would have the top down and let the sun and sea air bring us to an all time high. That, and singing with the radio at the top of our lungs...well, we would feel like kids again." At first Stacie smiled at that, then, visualizing her goofy parents, gave her eyes a roll and her head a little shake. She still had all the 'teen years' to go through with her own daughters before she'd be there.

Along the way we noticed most of the cars had Florida tags. The snowbirds had deserted the summer heat and returned to their northern homes. Locals were mowing their lawns and walking their dogs. The occasional smell of barbeque drifted through the window. Staring out at the water, I watched two people enjoying a thrill ride on a wave runner. Seeing people having such normal Sunday activities made me wish my Sunday could have been playing out in another way. The hospital entrance was just up ahead.

As we walked up we noticed some very happy folks coming out the doors. The patient was being wheeled out by a nurse as his family carried his totes of hospital goodies. One woman, looking like his daughter, carried the plastic bedpan. It seemed he had won the race, and she pompously held his trophy.

There were a couple more patients lined up, ready to make the great escape, but most looked like visitors. I'm sure I wasn't the only one who craved a different situation.

***

"Hi, Dad, it's Stacie. Mom and I made it."

"Hi, Bill." We pulled up chairs to each side of the bed and just stared at him. "You know, he seems a little pinker today. I wonder if the antibiotics are working and the pneumonia is getting better.

Stacie stared a little longer then agreed. "Yeah, he does. The other day he looked a little gray. I hope so."

After chatting over the top of Bill for about ten minutes, a nurse came in to check the machines and the IVs. Over the weekend there were so many new faces. Once I'd finally figured out all the nurses' names, they'd change. After introducing myself and Stacie, I asked how Bill was doing. She let me know that she really didn't know; she had only started her shift at three. I glanced up to the clock showing it was only three fifteen. "Oh. That's understandable. Is Dr. Grady here today?"

"Um, I believe so."

I decided not to ask anymore questions and see if he would show up. He'd probably be making rounds within the hour. Stacie began where we had left off, and I kept an eye on the blood pressure machine as we spoke.

I whispered, "Stacie, watch that machine." Even in my whisper it began to rise. I didn't want to do anything that would hurt Bill, but I couldn't help but be amazed with the results even when I spoke so softly.

"At home, Dad always had excellent hearing." I started to giggle. "He could be in the office and I could be out on the porch talking on the phone and he always knew what I was talking about, weird, huh?"

"No, I remember Dad watching TV in the living room while reading a book and still putting his two cents into a conversation I might be having with you in the kitchen. Do you remember?"

"Yes." We started to laugh, abruptly quieting before getting too loud. I felt silly and moved my lips forming the words without speaking, "Do... you... think... he... can... read... lips...?" We stifled our laughter one more time, calming down when a doctor entered the room.

This was the doctor who had liked all my cards and pictures on the wall. I recognized him but didn't know his name. Pointing to the collage, he commented again, "That is nice." Looking at Stacie, he asked. "Don't you think so?"

"Yes, of course."

I think he caught Stacie by surprise and was possibly a tiny bit flirtatious. Pretending I didn't notice, I wondered about Bill's condition. "How is the pneumonia? Bill's coloring looks better."

"Tests look good and we are considering taking him off the sedation today."

I jumped up, trying to maintain some composure. I barely could get the word out, "Today?"

"Yes. We have to get a specialist and staff to do this."

"Where's Dr. Grady? It's Sunday. I thought…"

"He'll be here shortly."

I became so tongue-twisted, and my heart felt like it would explode with the adrenaline that was pumping through. Teeter-tottering between fright and an anxiously awaited conclusion, I first seemed to have one foot glued to the ground then, like a flash, I felt I was higher than a kite.

"Wow!" *Was that all I could say at a time like this*, "Oh, my God! Thank you." The doctor could see he had obviously blown me away and needed to respond.

"Please, calm down. It will probably be at least an hour before we do the procedure. That's *if* we do the procedure."

'If', didn't sound good. I floated back to earth and decided to ignore that last phrase. "Okay. I think we'll just go take a walk for about fifteen minutes."

"That will be fine. See you in a little while."

Stacie and I headed outside. While I went to get coffee, she called her brother and sister to keep them informed. Seems both of them had gotten together and decided to drive down to see their dad. What ever their reason both of them felt they needed to be at Morton Plant Hospital. They had just left New Port Richey and would be at least another forty-five minutes. She was glad they were coming down to be with us, and so was I.

***

We re-entered the ICU to find a group of nurses and doctors conferring with one another. Dr. Grady had arrived and immediately began to explain what they had to do. I was given an option of being in or out of Bill's room; however, they hoped I would assist in keeping Bill calm when he awoke. I understood my role. Stacie observed from one side of the bed and I, the other. Like a play when the music begins, the curtains parted. I could see each of the staff brilliantly displaying their talents, and from the front row I nervously watched and awaited my cue.

Monitors and IV bags were examined as a table with sterile equipment was placed over the bed. Bill's arms and legs were restrained while the nurses and doctors checked and re-checked their procedures. They spoke a strange language; yet I understood as I watched.

Dr. Grady spoke, "Mrs. Faulkner, go ahead."

"Bill, I'm here honey. Open your eyes and you will see me. I am right here next to you. Don't try to speak, though. You are in a hospital and you have a tube in your mouth. Please, don't try to talk. Come on, sweetheart. Open your eyes." I repeated my words as the nurses detached tubes and replaced them with others. I glanced around only to see that they were all busy doing something. Stacie looked as though she was holding her breath with each word I spoke. Calmly, I continued. "Bill...?" His eyes fluttered and he followed my voice.

"Honey, I'm right here." Bill opened his eyes and for only a moment had that faraway stare. Then, like the glorious miracle that it was, he looked at me with such trust and love and to my surprise winked at me. "Oh, honey, I'm here and you can see me! I love you." I couldn't help crying. "Oh, don't try to speak yet." There is no word that could describe how wonderful I felt.

Stacie squealed and laughed out loud, crying with happiness. Bill looked over in her direction and blinked at her with his beautiful blue eyes. Gazing about the room, he returned his face to mine. "I love you," I told him again. Seeing the tears gently sliding down my cheek, a tiny frown brought his questioning eyebrows together. I explained to him again, very calmly, where he was and that it was so good to see him.

The doctors motioned that it was time to explain to Bill the next step. "Honey, listen to the doctor now. He needs you to listen." Bill focused on the doctor and seemed to be ready for whatever he had to say.

"Okay, Mr. Faulkner. I am going to take out the breathing tube that is in your mouth. On the count of three relax...exhale." I had no idea that it was so long. It came out very quickly.

Bill coughed only once and then looked back at me. He licked about his dry lips, and then very childlike, he puckered up for a kiss. I was very eager to kiss him and leaned as close as I was able. We kissed. Then we kissed again.

Bill spoke his first raspy words in over a week at five-eleven P.M. on May 15th, 2005. Slowly moving his eyes around the room he whispered, "I must be in Heaven."

Chapter 15

"Of course Dad did." I mentally reviewed the previous two hours and wondered. "I think he did, didn't he?" Shaye and I were sitting on the porch. Billy hadn't heard her comment as we walked out.

"Who did or didn't do what?" Billy asked from the kitchen. Shaye and I could hear a cork make its popping noise.

I spoke a little louder. "Shaye didn't think Dad knew her. Are you opening the wine?"

"Give me a second, Mom. Where do you keep the wine glasses?"

"They're over the fridge." I got up to help Billy. Together we walked back out to the porch, setting three glasses on the table. Billy poured. Raising them high, we touched them together, *clink*. Looking at Billy and Shaye with a great big grin, I took a deep breath and toasted, "Hallelujah! He's awake."

"This has absolutely been the week out of Hell. Oh, my God, it's just so awesome," Shaye replied and tasted her wine. We all sat with corny smiles. I'm sure they were thinking the same as I. *What a miracle!*

Billy spoke up. "When Dad asked me what had happened, I wasn't sure if I should tell him. It just came out. I told him he'd had a ruptured brain aneurysm. He made a face and said, 'Whew, that's bad.' I felt like he understood."

Propping my feet up on the empty chair, I agreed. "I saw that, too. Your dad did show concern and he said, 'Gees, I'm lucky."

Shaye, rethinking her suspicions, "Well, maybe he was just overwhelmed. You know, all that was going on with the doctors and stuff. I just had this feeling he wasn't recognizing me. I'm okay."

"Honey, don't worry. I'm sure he remembers his baby girl." I patted her hand. "When you have a chance to talk to him, you'll feel better.

"Speaking of baby girls, I hope Stacie got home safe?" She had left earlier from the hospital, wanting to get home before dark. Answering myself, "I'm sure she did." Then, with a burst of joy I couldn't contain, I yelled, "God, thank you! I am the happiest woman in the world!"

Shaye chimed in, "Praise God!"

I sang the rest. "From whom all blessings flow." I felt like I could hear the choir singing in the old church that I'd attended as a kid. What a long week. The wine was making me feel a little giddy. I was so happy that my sweetheart had come back. It was just so really great, finally feeling like I could relax. The kids and I rehashed the day's glorious events as we munched on some snacks. Slowly winding down, we had failed to realize it was after ten o'clock.

Shaye stood up, "I better get going or Brian's going to think I fell off the face of the earth."

"Okay, drive carefully. I'll talk to you tomorrow." I stood up to give her a hug and kiss. After she kissed her brother goodbye, I walked her to the front door. I waved as she pulled out of the driveway and then went back to the porch. "Do we dare have one more glass?" I asked Billy.

"Sure, we can celebrate a little." We sat watching the ripples on the pool that the sweet summer breeze was making, enjoying the wonderful evening and all our blessings. The roaring giant that had been blaring inside our heads all week had finally quieted and was at rest. Well, almost.

I entered the kitchen and grabbed the phone, telling Billy, "Before it gets too late I want to call and see how he's doing." His expression showed understanding as I dialed the numbers and was transferred to the ICU nurses' desk. That nurse then rang the nurse assigned to Bill.

"Hello, may I help you?"

"Yes, I'm Valerie Faulkner, and I just wanted to check on my husband, Bill."

"He's doing fine. I just fed him some stew, and I'm getting ready to wash him up."

"Stew – he loves stew. That's great!" My common sense knew better, but I had to ask, "May I talk to him?"

"No, sorry. But I'll give him a message."

I realized I sounded like a moron but continued, "Tell him I love him, and I'll be there in the morning."

"Okay. Goodnight."

"Good nigh…" I looked at the phone. "I guess she was done. Oh, well. It sounds like everything is okay. Dad ate stew."

Billy raised his hand to give me high five and said, "Very cool!"

"Yup, I think so, too." I placed the phone back on the receiver and gave Billy a hug and kiss. "I'm going to go color my hair and take a shower. Do you need anything?"

"No, Mom. I'm good. I think I'll turn in, too. Goodnight."

"Goodnight, Son. I love you."

"Love you too, Mom."

***

By the time morning came, I had only one goal in mind. I needed to get to the hospital A.S.A.P. Kathie offered to drive me down, and I was hurrying to be ready when she came. I had about five minutes left. Combing out the right side of my hair, I finished my braid. "There, that looks good." My makeup was perfect. I checked myself out in the mirror. The only thing I found disconcerting were the stubborn dark circles under my eyes that had become a permanent part of me during the week. I patted on a few more dabs of Oil of Olay. I just stepped away from the mirror. It was easier not to look at myself. My jeans pulled up with ease, and I ran my feet into my sandals. "Okay, I'm ready." Running downstairs I stopped and stood on the scale. "Wow, down five pounds."

The doorbell rang and I greeted Kathie, who had owned with her own business and now was elected to the Pasco County School Board. After so many years of working and meeting deadlines, she was always very prompt. I smiled, "Let me get my pocketbook. I'm ready to go." She could see I was on top of things. I silently praised myself for being on time. All my life I didn't bother to wear a watch, never worrying about exact minutes. Today was an exception; I felt like I was going on a date.

***

When the two of us entered Bill's room, he had one leg slung over the rail, and I rushed to cover up his naked body parts. Any attempt to disguise my uneasiness was not working and my voice quavered as I tried to greet Bill. "Well, hello, honey." I hoped Kathie had not seen more than she wanted to. I leaned over to give Bill a kiss, and he put his hand on my breast. Whispering through clenched teeth, I told him, "Kathie is with me." He ignored my statement and grabbed at the front of my jeans. Speaking up, I told him with a forced smile,

116

"Bill, Kathie is here to visit! Say hi."

His train of thought momentarily refocused, he glanced at the visitor chair where she had seated herself. "Hi."

A tray of food was in front of him but had been pushed out of reach. I asked if he wanted something to eat. When he nodded, I fixed his sheet and brought his breakfast closer. His hand shook as he attempted to lift his fork. "Bill, would you like me to help you?" Ignoring me, he abruptly threw the fork down. He grabbed a handful of scrambled eggs and shoved them into his mouth, locking me straight in the eyes as he chewed them up. His gaping mouth showed all the egg he had inside, as though he wanted to make sure I wasn't missing anything. As he stretched out his tongue, Kathie and I could see the half-chewed food. With his mouth still full he shoveled in some toast and reached for his coffee. I watched as his hand shook; he spilled half of the coffee that sloshed over him and his breakfast tray. I went to help him, but he gave me a defiant glare.

I couldn't help myself. I leaned in to sop up the coffee with some paper napkins. I was sure Kathie felt a need to attempt some diversion. As she searched in vain for something to say, I struggled to unlatch Bill's grip on the front of my shirt. When I was finally able to release his hold on me, he threw off his covers and exposed himself. I felt like I was dealing with a rowdy child.

Kathie stayed for an awkward half hour, watching as I tried to minimize the chaos that was occurring. She could see I was having quite some difficulty. Bill finally seemed preoccupied with the bedrail, and I sat down in the chair for a breather. Kathie's expression could be easily read. I knew what she was thinking. Somewhat scared, I knew what I was thinking.

"No, honey, stop that! Bill, take your hand away from there – you're going to get hurt!" He let go of the rail, and it came slamming down. "How did you do that? Shit, Bill. I don't know how to get it up."

Nurse Michelle entered to my rescue. She brought the rail up and tightened his arm restraints. "Hello," she acknowledged me and my sister. "He's like 'Peck's Bad Boy' and not just this morning. The night shift had their hands full."

I wasn't sure how to respond to her statement. Of course, I was sorry that my husband was being a pain. Didn't she have any compassion? Look what he had gone through.

"Well, he'll be off to sleep in no time. He needs to stay calm." I watched as she replaced his IV bag. Within minutes Bill was sleeping like a baby. Kathie left to go home. I spent most of the day watching my hubby rest peacefully.

With late afternoon approaching, Dr. Grady entered just as Bill was awakening.

"Hello, Mr. Faulkner. My name is Dr. Grady. Do you remember me?" Bill didn't show much enthusiasm toward the doctor, instead reached out to grope my body. Gently placing his hand in mine, I tried to make sure Bill wouldn't touch me inappropriately in front of the doctor. "Mr. Faulkner, do you know who this lady is?"

Bill sighed as though he were being bothered and answered, "Val."

"And what is she to you?"

Bill didn't seem to want to talk to him, just stared at Dr. Grady as though he were the one with problems. Bill reluctantly answered the next few questions.

"Okay, one last question. Do you know what year it is?"

Bill let out a deep breath. He acted as though he couldn't believe the doctor was bothering him this way. Understanding Dr. Grady was just trying to see how Bill's brain was doing, I prompted Bill to answer.

Dr. Grady, all right with my intervention, asked again, "So, can you tell me what year we are in?"

With a sarcastic tone of voice, Bill responded sharply, "It's 1985."

Chapter 16

At the fire place

There were so many things I should have been doing. Instead I was so involved with my stories: I was a bit preoccupied.

"The phone's been quiet." I was still sitting at the kitchen table. I reread that last sentence, 'It's 1985.' I couldn't help but chuckle. "Did I write anymore about that?" I checked another one of my folders. From under the table, Jake stirred and wondered who I was talking to.

"It's just me, Jake. I've finally gone crazy and I'm talking to myself."

I wasn't convinced this book thing was for me. I did have a few good parts, though. "Oh, here it is, 1985, just a few notes." I read out loud, "I asked Bill, "How old are you?"

"Oh, I'm about thirty-five." Tilting his head, he pondered, "Yeah, Thirty-five."

"How old do you think I am?"

"About, thirty-two."

"God, I wish." I smiled.

That was a treasured moment. Anytime he wanted to think I was thirty-two would be fine with me. He thought the kids were the same age as he and I. They weren't too happy about that but didn't overreact. Joyce did. When he acted as if he didn't know my sister, she got upset, thinking it was because she didn't look the way she had in 1985. I recall telling her, "No. He's just out of it."

"I wonder if she got over that," I sighed, "Poor Joyce."

I had a lot of time to think about everything that was happening then. It was not at all what I could or would have imagined. I was dreadfully tired and bewildered. The doctors had told me what I might expect on the first day Bill came to the hospital. I wasn't stupid; I comprehended what they said. They had given me an upfront, probable, detailed scenario of how life might be if Bill survived. But I don't think I ever really believed it.

Could anyone have accepted their theory and all their explanations with any real conviction? I stared at the box of folders, I certainly didn't! My problems had been placed in God's hands. I needed, more than ever, to keep the faith. I had wanted Bill to live and had sworn I would take care of him.

Jake was pawing at my leg from under the table. Lost in thought, thinking back on that day, I wasn't aware of the unconscious tapping sound of my pen against the table.

"Jake, do you want a cookie? Okay, just one. I don't want you getting fat and lazy, old boy." Jake followed me to the pantry. "All right, just two."

Sitting back down, I reached for a blank sheet of paper, pen in hand. "God, give me some help here, please."

***

Bill gently snored and the clock quietly ticked. I had been sitting in the chair for about four hours, just watching him, wondering about the two of us and what we were going to do. The drone of machines and beeping noises monotonously filled the background. Coming and going, the nurses continued to take very good care of Bill's needs. I was too worn out for even the smallest of conversations; I assumed they understood as they left me to myself, deep in my own thoughts. Each day, family members brought me to the hospital and picked me up. I was so grateful for their help, but this rough road was mine to travel alone. I wondered if I could.

Over time, the nurses informed me of Bill's shocking behavior, and I came to my own conclusions: it was easier for them to keep him sedated than attempt to control him. I would wait all day for just a few moments with him until he'd zone out to 'Bill's World' all by himself. I would be left behind to sit, hour after hour, in the visitor's chair.

I thought about what Dr. Grady had said, almost compassionately. Informing me I would need to be patient, he suggested, "Repeat the stories you and your husband are familiar with. How you met, your marriage, your children, your grandchildren." I knew I would if he were alert. I tried to fit in as much as I could on the occasions Bill was awake and aware of my presence, but I felt like there just weren't enough moments. Complaining to Dr. Grady, his standard response seemed to be, "Get some rest, Mrs. Faulkner. I know this is hard on you." I felt so frustrated.

Nurse Michelle was the one who, at first, I wasn't sure I even liked. Her businesslike demeanor and aloof persona made her seem cold and hard-hearted. In reality, she was dedicated to her work; just had a shortfall when it came to bedside manner. Seeing how stressed I had become, her restrained compassion for Bill and me broke free. She explained how Bill, being so physically strong, combined with his aggressiveness, was not good. He could hurt himself or someone else. "With a brain injury of this magnitude, we need to take it slow and gradually discover the best way to assist in his recovery."

I had an idea and explained it to Nurse Michelle. I must have been convincing as I told her how strong our bond was. I believed if I could be with him for longer periods of time, I could be of help. She relayed this to the doctors, requesting that Bill have less sedation while I was at his bedside. In this 'new' Michelle, I discovered a sensitive, caring person who had opened a door and allowed me in.

Grateful for her input, I was so happy to spend one whole hour with my husband.

The first thing I did was turn the TV to a music only channel, a soft rock station instead of CNN news the staff had on. Bill and I usually listened to country music, but this would suffice. It was fun to hear the oldies after so long, and they brought back loads of memories. Bill immediately perked up listening to the music. He sang along with the Beach Boys, not missing a word of 'Help Me, Rhonda.' This was encouraging. Bill was always good with music trivia. I grinned from ear to ear when he acted as though he was ready for a game. Often he had quizzed me about song titles and their artists; I was thrilled when his first question was, "Who sang that?"

I knew who did but wanted to know if he did. I asked, "Who?" More than once he was able to find the correct answer. I sang with him and spoke about our family. I took his hands in mine and prayed with him. I reminisced with him, our life together as partners. Day by day, hour after hour, moment to moment, we spent precious time attempting to bring back the lost files in his mind.

Not realizing it, my mothering nature grew stronger and stronger. Perhaps I was facilitating him, for I strictly abided by the rules given us and didn't notice the transition that was taking place. With each day that passed, Bill's personality grew more and more challenging. Some things were coming back to him while other things were vague; it became harder to communicate. From one breath to the next, he would whine at me and then, as if the devil were inside of him, he would disregard any respect and growl with shameful contempt. I didn't know if Bill remembered being the head of his household, a king on his throne. Now he was like a child, an uncontrollable child. Certainly he needed help, but most of the time his attitude reminded me of that old saying: Mother, please...I'd rather do it myself.

Someone needed to take control of our situation and face the monsters one by one. In order for us to survive, I had to assume responsibility. I needed to realize that our once fairy-tale life had been obliterated by the bomb that went off in Bill's head.

Each day concentrating on something new, we took baby steps forward. It was difficult when we would slide back to the beginning. When Bill moved ahead, even if it was something small like remembering the Beach Boys, I would smile. I would smile because I knew God was doing something, even if I wasn't quite sure what.

I spoke to God constantly and gave praise for the slightest improvements. Yet the hurdles I had to jump reminded me regularly that Bill's goals were far from reached. One step forward, three back. They were small victories until the seizures started.

***

Taking a break down on the outdoor patio, Mark and I ran into each other and found comfort in some conversation. Having so much in common, we shared our daily battles and concerns over a cup of coffee, enjoying a few moments of feeling sane. The short break from our confinement and the fresh air was only a temporary fix. We had our jobs to do, and it felt like break time ended all too soon. Knowing we were needed, we headed back up to the fifth floor together. We entered the ICU and marched back to our sentry posts; he in one direction, I the other.

Entering the room, I found a new nurse attending Bill. I introduced myself. She told me her name was Katherine. I immediately thought to myself, *I'll be able to remember that one.*

"Our granddaughter's name is Katherine. Bill, did you hear that?"

She was busy giving Bill a sponge bath, and he was giving her a hard time in return. Katherine didn't pause from her duties to chat. Bill, hearing my voice, took one look at me and ceased his fussing. I gave him a kiss and stood at his bedside. I didn't know if his behavior would stay calm or if he would suddenly react to me negatively. For the moment he was being good. He watched me as I spoke to her, telling her of all that had occurred. He appeared interested in what I was saying.

She appeared somewhat frazzled and with a breathless arrogance tattled miserable tales of Bill. She didn't try to conceal her feelings at all and acted as if Bill couldn't understand. Katherine explicitly explained one annoyance after another, and I couldn't help but wonder if Bill was an isolated case. *Had all the other patients that woke up with similar diagnoses been perfect angels?* I doubted that, but judging by her remarks and body language, he must have been pretty unique.

I watched as she tried to dress him in pajama bottoms. Clearly, her work was just a job; it seemed she would have preferred to be somewhere else. I grimaced along with my husband. Bill had a catheter with a bag. My thoughts concluded it would have been easier to keep him in one of the hospital gowns. He groaned and pulled up his feet as she tugged and yanked at his legs, his struggling making her task impossible.

I could feel the grimace on my own mouth, ready to say "Eek." Although I didn't want to butt in, I had to say something. Straining to remain calm, I spoke through my teeth, "Please, Katherine, I think he'd prefer not to have those pants on."

"Well, I am not having much luck. You can see that. I think he should have his pajama bottoms on!" I thought she sounded a tad sarcastic to me, and I really didn't want to make a scene. Looking at her, I spoke with a little lighter note, trying to appeal to her humorous side.

"Bill always sleeps naked. I know he'd rather be naked, but I'm sure I could convince him to wear the shirt." She continued without hesitating. Presuming she didn't think either of us was funny or cute, I felt agitated that Katherine was ignoring me. I can get a stubborn streak occasionally, and I contemplated what to say next. Maybe an hour from now I'd have a perfect reply, but now...nothing. I could feel heat sparking in my cheeks as my mind ran rampant. If only I could organize all the nasty thoughts running through my head. Bill was always much quicker when it came to witty comebacks. I remembered our teamwork and looked at his face. *'Bill, come up with something, quick!'* At that moment Bill was having a seizure.

While all this petty nonsense about wearing bottoms or not was taking place, he was having a seizure. I was speechless. I didn't want to act like a know-it-all or, worse yet, panic, so I gently spoke, "He's having a seizure." She fought his trembling legs. *Had she heard me?* Louder and with a brisk pat on her arm I said, "Katherine...Katherine! Bill's having a seizure!" She glared at me for disturbing her and looked at Bill. By now his eyes were shut and he lay completely still. "I saw it... he was having a seizure! His legs and arms and body were shaking! You didn't see that? You couldn't feel that?"

"I'm sure I would have noticed that, Mrs. Faulkner." She leaned towards his face and examined him with a much keener eye. Looking back at me she said, "Looks like he's sleeping to me."

I resented her arrogance; I was pissed! Without saying a word, I gave her a look that could kill. I ran my fingers through Bill's hair. His face felt moist. He lay motionless. Frightened, I watched his chest as his breathing let his lungs swell and knew I needed to find someone who would explain and reassure me he was okay.

I waited for the right moment, and when the doctor came in, the one without a name, I told him about Katherine. He checked the book outside the room and reassured me Bill couldn't have had a seizure, nothing was written up about it. I stared at him with anguish and clearly spoke each word decisively. "This is what I am saying. The nurse on duty didn't see it, I did! She was too busy putting on his pajamas!"

He stared down at me, and leaning closer, he brought up the question, "What exactly did you see?" Describing in full detail, I told him accurately what had happened. He informed me that this indeed was a seizure. "It sounds like a petit mal. There's nothing petite about it though; it's a type of seizure that can occur suddenly and without reason." Doctors came in to discuss the seizures. Tests proved Bill would need to be on extra medication until these incidents stopped, *if they stopped.*

A valuable lesson had been learned. Katherine taught me to watch everybody with an underlying scrutiny. If I needed to be by Bill's bed side twenty-four/seven... I would. I strived for every bit of information I could, and if I didn't find justifiable explanations, I asked again and again. I couldn't allow myself to be naïve, not now.

Chapter 17

Putting one foot in front of the other was an effort. When Kathie and Dave dropped me off at the house, I could hardly wave my goodbyes. Inside, I couldn't wait to kick off my shoes. I sat down on the couch and thought about how peaceful and quiet it was. I was bushed and just wanted to veg out for awhile.

I noticed the dirt that had accumulated under the television. Like a zombie, I sat there staring as the dust bunnies multiplied. I had to let go of the day's events. I casually thought about making dinner, but since Billy wasn't home, there was no urgent need to start. Fleetingly, I considered vacuuming. "Nah…"

I wished I could calm down just a little. That nurse Katherine was monopolizing my thoughts. Filled to the brim with contempt for her, I couldn't stand it. Why had she ignored me? I felt like screaming, but what good would it do? Everything was so overwhelming. I felt burned out.

Hearing the garage door open, I realized Billy was home. He had gone to buy materials to remodel the garage bathroom. *He told me he was going to do that,* I remembered. *Good, I remembered something.*

Bang…! Bang…!

The sound was coming from the garage. I needed to mend my frayed emotions before investigating. I'd find out what was going on soon enough. I recalled my mom saying when we were kids, "I need to take twenty minutes." Suddenly that made sense. My curiosity got the best of me though, and after about ten minutes I got up, started the coffee maker, and headed in the direction of the back door.

Billy yelled as I entered, "I didn't know you were home! Watch your step." Looking down I could see broken up concrete and stacks of two by fours.

"I got home about five. I was just taking a few minutes...how are you doing?" I coughed from the dust.

"I'm bringing the new wall out to here for the shower." He pointed with his foot. "It will be handicapped-accessible, in case Dad needs a walker or a wheelchair..."

I knew my expression could have showed more enthusiasm. I really was so proud of my son for having such a good heart, but I couldn't bear the thought of Bill needing a special shower. Vivid thoughts flooded my head, and I couldn't hold back my anguish. "Umm...that will be..." Muttering, I turned to go back in the house; the tears had started. I hoped he hadn't noticed.

Billy dropped his hammer and yelled, "Aw, Mom. Come on, we need to prepare."

Quickly wiping my eyes, I turned back to him, my voice wavering, "I know. It's just been such a rough day."

He knows it was like all the others. He's on the same page as I am and just trying to bring some hope into our lives.

Consciously, I made an effort to watch him work. So much like his dad, building things came naturally. I could see he was making progress. I stepped over and around all the debris on the floor to stand closer to him. "Let me give you a hug." Brushing off saw dust, he reached over to put his arm around my shoulder. As lightheartedly as I could manage I said, "Thanks, son." Sighing, "This is probably a good idea."

I couldn't help but think about Bill, the way he meticulously put things together. He never did anything on a hunch or without a plan.

I told Billy, "I'll get dinner ready while you play."

"Okay, Mom. I'm getting hungry." Preparing our dinner I couldn't help but remember the 'good old days, back when.'

Bill and I had enjoyed working many hours on schemes and designs; some small, some large, projects had been plentiful in a house with so many rooms.

I laid the chicken out on the broiler pan and set the timer on the oven for forty minutes. Setting fresh vegetables out on the counter, I found the cutting board and a knife. I wondered if Billy liked onions. I grabbed the big salad bowl and stuck my head out in the garage. "Do you like onions in your salad?"

"Yeah, I like them. What are you making?"

"Baked chicken, salad, you know, easy dinner. It'll be a little while yet." I checked the clock. "Maybe twenty minutes, okay?"

"Sure. I have plenty to do out here." I went back to dinner prep and searched for the salad dressing in the cluttered fridge.

***

I thought about the wall behind our refrigerator. We had a painted heart inscribed, 'Bill loves Val;' the last time we did it, we used musky yellow and sage colored paints. God, that was just after the New Year. Who would have thought...?

When we built this house we had been married for about ten years. By then we had accumulated a number of newspaper clippings and magazine articles of dreamy homes and landscapes. Cool children's rooms with no signs of hand-me-down furnishings; exquisite kitchens with updated appliances and modern gadgets. Our files had grown quite plump. As we sorted through our paper dreams, we discovered the picture

131

of this house.

Bill and I knew right away that the home was meant for us. Smoothing out the curled up edges of the newsprint photo, we revealed the house plan code number and address of where we could order the blueprints. I waited for the mailman anxiously for weeks until we were finally notified that the plans were no longer available. I was so disappointed. Bill said, "Never fear, I took drafting in high school. I'll draw up a plan."

With onion skin paper, a ruler, t-square, and a pencil he set out to accomplish his task. For the next six months, he drafted the plans to our home, making it look just like the picture on the outside and designing the rooms on the inside. I was amazed at how professional the drawings looked. Sometimes we would design together into the wee hours of the night. So many times we walked through our new home on that pencil drawing. We were familiar with every inch of our paper house.

Building it would be much different and became quite a challenge. We were appreciative God didn't throw his hands up and abandon us. This was a humongous job for novices. After we cleared the land, spring came and Bill began to build, stick by stick. Coordination of each phase threw us into a whirlwind of schedules and decisions. Being meticulous, Bill prepared and planed for each day's work. I'd bring him lunch and examine each freshly constructed wall with exuberance. I don't think either of us realized how much work would be involved, but gradually the wood went up and the rooms took shape. There were only a handful of glitches in the whole house. When I suggested one exterior wall should have a bigger window, he was able to maintain a sense of humor. Winking at me, he said, "Sure, I can do that. But you'll need a change order, lady, and it's going to cost you big time." I giggled, wrapping my arms around him. I knew what that meant. I blushed, thinking about paybacks...

When it was finished, the Faulkner residence stood thirty feet tall. A two-story frame home with wood decks and porches, huge eat-in-kitchen, four bedrooms, tiled bathrooms and a fireplace, certainly not anything you'd picture in Florida; more like Maine or Vermont.

***

Wow, that was over twenty-five years ago. I had the table set and went to take a peek at the garage. *The smell of fresh sawn wood always brought back these memories. Like little greeting cards from God.*

"Billy, dinner's ready."

It was a quiet meal. Billy was thinking about the bathroom, and I was thinking about Bill. After a couple of cookies for dessert, I told him, "I'll take care of the dishes. I know you want to go build a bathroom."

I cleaned up the kitchen as quickly as I could so I could call the hospital. I had been thinking about Bill since I'd come home. I got through to Bill's nurse and listened to her complaints. That was the first of many calls. *I wonder if all of the nurses are like Katherine. Are they provoking his bad behavior?*

By midnight I had spoken to at least six different nurses, and none gave me any good news. I asked if I should drive back to be with Bill, but they all discouraged me. Fretting, I vacillated from one thought to the next. Thirty-five miles away from my husband, yet I felt like he was on another planet. I couldn't bare the thought of all these 'alien creatures' being responsible for him: the man they couldn't stand.

I complained to my 'Pillow Bill'; I complained to God. I staggered from too little sleep and listened to my heart thump. My eyes couldn't stay shut; they couldn't stay open.

When I called at four o'clock in the morning, the nurse

on duty was a young man, and although I didn't get his name, he told me Bill was finally asleep.

"If there are any changes, we will call you. Go to bed, Mrs. Faulkner. Get some sleep!"

"Promise you'll call me?"

"Yes, I promise. Goodnight."

***

The ringing wouldn't end. I slapped the alarm clock, yelling "Shut up!" The lamp on the nightstand teetered as the clock radio crashed to the floor. Barely light outside, I squinted through sleepy eyes. "What the hell is going on?" Creeping to the edge of the bed, I reached down to shut it off, but it had stopped. "Shit, was I dreaming?"

Again, it began. The ringing sounds pierced my ears. I strained to open my eyes. "Oh my God, it's the phone." Tripping over the blanket, I dashed for the telephone. I made it by the fourth ring. "Hello?"

"Valerie? Is this Valerie?"

"Yes, this is Valerie, what?" My ear recognized the voice on the other end, but my brain couldn't place who it belonged to.

"This is Michelle from Morton Plant Hospital."

"Oh. Oh my God, what? Is Bill okay?"

"He's been up for hours and is asking for you. He's had a rough night, and he's going to have to be sedated again. I wanted to see if you could get down here soon. We may be able to hold off if you can keep him calm."

"I'll get there as quickly as I can! I'm over an hour away. Please wait for me – I'll hurry."

"We'll try. Be careful."

I hung up the phone and ran to the bathroom to splash water on my face. I grabbed my jeans from the day before, pulling them up as I hobbled to the side of the bed. I picked up the shirt I had thrown there yesterday and smelled it. As it went over my head, I persuaded myself this was faster than hunting for another. *Hurry*...I brushed my hair and braided it and ran downstairs for my shoes. Slipping into them I ran through the office and out to the garage. "Damn!" I realized the Jeep was not in there. It was parked in the driveway while the bath room construction was going on. I ran back to the kitchen and out the front door. I got to the Jeep and realized it was locked. "Would be a good idea to get my keys..." I ran back into the house and couldn't find them. I was frantic. I hadn't been driving for the past week and a half. "Where are my keys?" Suddenly I had this recollection of placing them in the junk drawer for safe keeping. "Yes", right where I left them, "Thank you, God!"

I dashed back out the front door and locked it behind me. I got in the driver's seat and started up the engine. When I put the shift in reverse, I remembered I didn't have my license. "Oh, crap, my brain isn't working!" I scolded myself, "I don't even have any money. I should leave a note for Billy, too." All over again I ran back in and then made the trek to head out, one more time. Before I got to the door, I knew I had forgotten my cigarettes!

Back in the kitchen I stopped and just stood still. At the cabinet, panting for air, I spoke, "Lord, I need your help." I leaned over the countertop and folded my hands. Taking long, deep breaths, I made myself stand still for just a minute longer. "God, please let me calm down and please take care of me. I am acting like a crazy maniac, and I need your help. I think I have everything now."

Then, whimpering, I asked, "Will you help me get to the hospital safely? And please let me drive carefully so I won't hurt anyone. Thank you."

***

As I put my seatbelt on I realized it had been ten minutes since Michelle had called. The Jeep's clock read five minutes after six, and I figured I couldn't get to the hospital much before seven-fifteen. That would be on a really good day.

"Hold on, Bill; I'm on my way..." Backing out of the driveway, I noticed that no one seemed to be up and about. The light from the rising sun could be seen, barely peeking through the tree limbs. The neighborhood was still tucked in. The city streets were vacant except for a scruffy little dog that poked around a fallen garbage can, snooping and sniffing for his morning snack. The tall street lights blinked off one after the other as the darkness surrendered to light.

Approaching my first major highway, I realized the traffic light about a quarter of a mile away had stopped all oncoming traffic. I said, "Thank you Lord, for a great start," and began my road trip. I was pleased to have this impressive break since U.S. Highway 19 never slept. I traveled at about 45 mph, the safest speed limit for this area. As I drove I noticed in my rearview mirror that the cars behind me weren't catching up. They remained a good 20 car lengths behind swarming like bees.

Then I noticed the vehicles in front of me were about 20 or 30 car lengths ahead. I moved along at a steady pace; never catching up to them. It was as though I was in a serene bubble drifting on glorious wings. If that was not strange enough, I was in awe when I realized there were no cars beside me. I was driving on three lanes of highway; no other cars. I thought to myself, *Thank you Lord, this is great!* During my miraculous ride, I was like a single link in a chain that remained unconnected from all the others. I owned the road. From behind as well as up ahead, the cars jockeyed as they all scrambled for the pole position. From my bubble I viewed brake lights blinking far ahead. One after the other the criss-crossing automobiles changed lanes in their hurried ritual. The tiny red lights looked like a digital sign and I considered their message. *The Man upstairs cares...*

"I love you, Lord; this is wonderful. Yet, I have to admit that this is very weird."

When I reached Holiday, I had completed one third of my trip and laughed out loud. I giggled as I fiddled with the knobs to turn the radio on. I found my country music station and listened to my favorite songs. Singing along at the top of my lungs, I was pleased that, for a weekday, so many songs were the ones played regularly on Rise-Up. I knew them well. Then, in between were sentimental love songs, the ones Bill and I had always enjoyed. It felt as though during certain songs God's voice was singing just for me. With others, I clearly heard Bill's voice serenading me from afar. I drove along and thought about what the tire cover on the back of the Jeep proclaimed: LIFE IS GOOD. Isn't that the truth?

Any confusion or fears of losing my way diminished. I had plenty of time to recognize the avenues I needed to turn onto as well as enjoy the tenderness of a morning awakening. I gladly waved, Good morning, world! My hair blew in the wind and my spirit took flight. Hope for a better day was as secure as the grip I placed on the steering wheel.

You guided me Lord. You turned dozens of traffic lights green when I approached. You gave me three red lights, just enough time to gather my wits.

I pulled into the hospital at six-forty, an unforgettable thirty-five minute ride. "Father, no one is ever going to believe me when I tell them. You rode as my copilot all the way to Clearwater."

Bowing my head, I raised my hands. "Thank you, God. I do...I do believe!"

Chapter 18

Almost running, I entered the hospital and made a quick right through the emergency room doors. I knew there was always hot coffee waiting on the visitor's table. Snagging a cup, I headed down the hall for the elevator. I juggled my purse and coffee as I pushed the 'up' button with my elbow and then stood back. "Come on..." I could see the down arrow blinking on top of the elevator casement and waited impatiently for the doors to open. The coffee steamed and I wanted to taste it, but it had to cool off a little. I tapped my foot on the tile floor and blew into the Styrofoam cup.

I started getting goose bumps. The air conditioning was so cold. There aren't many visitors this early in the morning to heat the place up. It was strange seeing it so deserted.

The doors opened. I pushed number five and they closed.

"Umm...this is really, really good," the tiny sip of coffee tasted hot and strong and as good as what I brewed at home. The elevator halted, surprising me when the doors opened wide on the third floor.

A woman in a white smock, carrying some charts on her arm and standing in the hallway hesitated and held the doors open. "Going up?"

"Yes, I'm going to the fifth floor." I answered.

"Never mind, I'm headed in the other direction I'll get it on the way down." The huge doors closed again, and I waited for them to open on five. Exiting the elevator, I walked promptly up to the huge double doors that would let me into the ICU and pushed the button. Automatically, they opened and I entered as fast as I could. I hurried down the corridor, being careful not to spill my coffee.

I looked into Bill's room. Nurse Michelle was standing next to the blood pressure machine, logging stats on a note-pad. Bill looked as though he was resting but opened his eyes as I entered.

"I made it! Good morning, honey; hi, Michelle." My mind was running rampant in preparation of telling them about my drive down. I placed my pocketbook on the chair and gave Bill a big kiss. Leaning back up, I looked at him closer,

"Sweetheart, are you okay?"

"He's probably getting a little groggy; we had to…"

I gulped and just stood there biting my lip; I couldn't say a single word. *Only in my mind I screeched, "Had to! Baloney! You could have given me the time I needed to get here. I only talked to you at ten minutes before six."* I looked up at the clock and the hands showed ten to seven. I looked back at her*, "It's been one hour. I got dressed, I drove here, and I'm in this room.* I told you I was coming!*"*

"I'm sorry, Doctor's orders."

I plopped down in the chair next to Bill's bed and tried to suppress my anger. I cupped a hand over my mouth to restrain myself. I felt the heat of my repressed emotions searing my stoic expression.

Bill was oblivious to our conversation. I was glad he had smiled for me, but he was already having difficulty keeping his eyes open. He reached out to hold my hand and clasped very tightly. It actually hurt. *Did he think I'd leave him again?*

Michelle finished and went to the desk outside the room. I could feel Bill's grip loosening and held his hand until his strength faded. Stroking his arm, I watched as a quiet sleep fell upon him. On his back, his tummy looked so flat. He had obviously lost weight. I reached over to let my hand rub his stomach gently. Feeling a band at his midsection I peeked under the coverlet to inspect. Bill had a canvas type material belt on. I looked closer. It was about four inches wide and was connected with a Velcro closure at his back. Thinner bands connected to each side of the belt were fastened under the bed.

"When did they put this on?" I whispered to myself. I looked out at Michelle to check her progress. I had an urge to stand up and stomp my feet for drugging Bill, but I still wanted to tell someone of my journey. I had planned to tell Michelle. Diligently, she flipped through pages, scribbling in her information.

From the corner of my eye I noticed a red sign on the outside of the glass window. I hadn't seen it there before. It was a printed page that had two large eyeballs on it, and I strained to read what it said. I spelled it out loud from left to right, "k-s-i-R- l-l-a-F." I thought for a second, and realized I was seeing it backwards, "Duh...Fall Risk!"

I looked back at Bill all tied down. Leaning back in the chair, I folded my hands behind my neck and exhaled, putting the puzzle pieces together. "You tried to get out of bed, didn't you?"

"Excuse me, Michelle. I'm going to go downstairs. You have my cell phone number – call me if Bill wakes up, okay?"

She looked up at me over the top of her glasses. "I will. He'll probably be out for awhile."

In the cafeteria, I bought a banana and a yogurt to take outside. The usual cashier lady wasn't at her register. *Who can I tell?* Out on the smoker's patio I sat down at my table to enjoy my breakfast. I was the only one there. It was so pleasant outdoors except for a ray of sun that beamed right at my face, blinding me. I scooted my chair so I would not be bombarded head on. From that point of view, a number of people inside a gated area about forty feet away could be seen. I wasn't close enough to hear them but recognized their laughter. *It must be a gathering place for the community of hospital people. They seem so calm and happy.*

With time to spare, I checked in with Billy. He was on his way to a job and told me he'd call me back. I called my sister Joyce, who was frantically getting ready to take Mom and Dad to get their monthly medical exam by nine. Shaye was already at work, and I got her answering machine. I figured Stacie would still be in bed, so I didn't call. She was only on her second day of summer break. I couldn't do that to her.

I was surprised when the chair next to me slid out, scraping on the pavement. "Oh, Mark...hi."

"You're early this morning," he answered. I could smell the fresh scent of Downy fabric softeners coming from him. "Are you going to be out here for a little while?"

"Yes."

"Good, then I'll get us some coffee and be right back."

"Thank you." I watched him go through the emergency room doors and could see him returning in no time at all.

When he sat down we filled each other in on our spousal dramas, and when I had the opportunity, I told him of my journey. I think it strummed a cord deep down inside him. I didn't have any trouble recognizing the spirit within him. I could see his aqua eyes filling with tears. On a lighter note I began, "And that's what I've been up to this morning." I appreciated his warm, encouraging smile and the sincere look in his eyes that let me know he enjoyed my story. Standing up, "I really better get back up to Bill."

"I'll walk with you." He stood and we both pushed our chairs in.

About every hour and a half Mark and I would go share some down time on the patio. His wife was sedated most of the time, and Bill was still out cold. It was nice to have some-one who understood.

When I got back to the room after one of my jaunts, I dis-covered Bill awake. A therapist was getting him ready for his first attempt at standing. He was a young man, who seemed to be of Asian heritage and yet spoke English very well. His ac-cent gave me no trouble as he explained what he planned to do. My biggest concern was that he was, at most, five feet tall, and I wondered how such a small man would be able to assist Bill. I didn't get in his way, but my legitimate concern had me hovering at Bill's bedside. I was thinking about the red sign with eyeballs. I watched as he helped Bill to sit up, placing his legs over the side of the bed; I kept still and remained quiet. Calmly speaking to Bill, he explained each task and Bill co-operated. When Bill's feet reached the floor, he looked as though he was balanced on a wobbling ladder next to the therapist. The young man stood eye level with Bill's chest. Bill hadn't even straightened out his legs. The therapist coaxed Bill to stand upright, making attempts to guide him to a standing position. Bill refused, keeping his legs bent at the knees.

Turning his head to me he said, "He very strong." Bill's stance was strange, and glancing downward, I realized Bill was solidly standing on his catheter hose. I tried not to panic, but I could see that this explained Bill's bent position. Drops of blood were falling to the floor from under his gown. I leaned down to see what I could do, telling the therapist I needed to move the hose out from under Bill's foot. The therapist assisted in holding up Bill's upper half.

I relocated the hose a few inches away from Bill's feet. Bill stood straight up and looking way down at the therapist, smiled. The therapist looked way up at him and said, "There, dat vas easy." I just stood there shaking my head at the two of them.

"Easy?" *(I'm all out of breath, and you guys thought that*

was easy?)

Bill was standing. Well, sort of. Clinging to his little friend, he swayed back and forth. He must have felt so good; looking over to me he said, "Okay, let's go home!"

I hadn't noticed Dr. Grady standing at the end of the bed and was startled when I heard, "Not yet, Mr. Faulkner." Bill turned his head towards the doctor, his knees buckling simultaneously. The therapist and I pushed Bill to the edge of the bed, plopping his bottom down on the mattress.

Dr. Grady continued. "But I have good news. We are moving you out of ICU and giving you a room in the CCU. That's the critical care unit."

Bill didn't make a fuss like I would have imagined, and there was no more mention about going home. I asked what this meant. The doctor explained that leaving the ICU was like stepping up but in reality not by much. Bill would share one nurse with about three other patients instead of the one on one care of the ICU. He continued, "Within the hour we will get you ready for the move." Dr. Grady glanced at his papers. "Ah, here it is. You will be in room 586-D."

"Does this mean I can stay?"

"Yes, Mrs. Faulkner. You can stay." He gave me a warm smile, and I thought I detected a little laugh. "We'll bring in a cot. They're not too comfortable." He waggled his hand in a so-so fashion, "Linens and a pillow, too, for you to sleep on."

I walked around the therapist and gave the doctor a hug. He didn't flinch at my affections this time as I told him, "Thank you. Thank you so much." Turning back to Bill, I felt like my heart would leap out of my chest. A silly grin froze on my face. Bill looked at me with raised eyebrows, his big blue eyes wide open. He formed a grin from cheek to cheek, mirroring mine. Keeping my excitement to a minimum, no jumping or shouting, I allowed myself a simple and to the point, "Yahoo!"

***

It took about two hours for the paper trail to be completed. At about five forty-five a crew came to relocate Bill. "Look, Bill, there *is* a world! It's been eleven days since you've seen anything other than the ICU. What do you think, pretty neat?" He just stared out the window in silent wonderment. His new room had a single bed and was much bigger than the ICU room. A great big window stretched from one side of the room to the other, viewing another wing of the hospital. Gazing from the fifth floor, one could see a lot of sky and clouds. A television mounted on brackets was located in the center of another wall about six feet from the floor. Two chairs welcomed from beneath the TV. A private bathroom containing a toilet and sink jogged out from the wall closest to the entrance. A folded cot was pushed up against the only bare wall in the room.

Within minutes a brunette nurse, a tiny, little thing weighing about ninety-five pounds, came in and told us she was going to walk Bill to the bathroom. "He hasn't walked yet." I said.

"Well, there's a first time for everything. Come on, Mr. Faulkner. Let's get you up and into the bathroom. I wondered what was she thinking, but Bill appeared excited with the notion. She explained how we would walk him and taught me how to hold his arm. I was really scared that he would be too big for the two of us, yet my opinion was not valued at this point. When we were ready, she spoke calmly to the both of us, "Okay, up you go." The three of us walked the fifteen feet or so; Bill putting one foot in front of the other with her coaching, and we made it to the bathroom door. The lesson continued, and we learned all the little safety techniques necessary to arrive at our destination alive. *Success!* I stopped holding my breath. She congratulated us on a job well done, and we repeated our stroll back to the bed. Looking at us both, she said, "You two will do great. Just stay away from Psychiatry." Abruptly, she left without an explanation.

***

An older woman in very neat business attire entered. The woman sat down in one of the arm chairs and proceeded to pull out her knitting. Her white curly hair, and plump figure gave her a grandmotherly appearance. I wouldn't have been surprised if she offered us a plate of home baked cookies. When she didn't say anything, I finally spoke up.

"My name is Valerie; this is my husband Bill." As she nodded at me I asked, "And...who are you?"

Resting her yarn and needles on her lap, she looked at me. "Annette." That's all she said.

"Oh. It's nice to meet you." *What did she want... why was she in the room?*

She then announced, "I'm a sitter."

"What's a sitter?"

"They didn't tell you?"

"Tell me what? No. No one told me anything."

"Sitters work in the hospital and watch the patients. Nurses can't be here all the time, so we watch for them." She paused, "And for you, too, when you want to take a break."

"Wow, I had no idea."

Annette smiled and picked up her knitting. Daylight was waning. The clock read bedtime for most of the patients. At all of eight thirty, the intercom announced visiting hours had ended.

Chapter 19

Annette helped me regain my trust in people. Who couldn't relate to a knitting Grandma? Although she was in the beginning stages of her project, it was already absolutely stunning. The detail in her threadwork showed years of experience. Bill was out like a light. There had been so many changes for him to adjust to; a new room and, for him, what must have been an exhausting workout. He wasn't snoring, but I could see he was in a sound sleep. I sat Indian style on the little cot I had opened up in the middle of the room. The bottom of Bill's bed was even with my head. Underneath, I could see where the safety straps were tied and the security system wires connected to his alarm. I watched him, then Annette. I watched the clock.

The hallways were clearing as it dawned on me, if I were going to have one last cigarette for the evening I had better do it soon. "Would you mind if I left to go have a cigarette?"

Not looking up, Annette answered, "Of course not, dear. Go, take your time. He's sleeping. If he wakes up, I'll tell him you'll be right back."

"Thank you."

When I arrived on the ground floor, the halls were empty, and it looked like some of the lights had been turned off. All the rooms coming off the hallway were closed up for the evening, the windowed doors showing only darkness inside. A tall, black man in a security uniform guarded the door ahead. As I approached the exit door that led to the smoker's patio, my shoes squeaked and echoed in the barren passage. I watched the man lock the door as the last visitor left. When I reached him, I asked, "Will I be able to get back in if I go out to have a cigarette?"

Looking down at me, he replied, "You will have to use the door on the other side of the main entrance, ma'am." He pointed about fifty yards away to a lighted side door. It was very dark in between. "There's a walk you can follow if you like," pointing in a different direction, he showed me where it started. This wasn't exactly what I wanted to do, and my brain raced for solutions.

"How about I just go out and come back to this door, and you can let me in?" My words sounded lame, I knew, immediately after I said them. Instinctively I tried to charm him with a silly smile.

"Sorry ma'am. Over there's the only way to get back in." I stared out the glass door and visions of getting locked out terrified me. My overzealous imagination visualized the creepy unknown of what might be waiting out there.

"Never mind." Pausing, I looked at him in hopes that he might change his mind. "Guess I'll have to wait until morning?"

Making no attempt to break any rules, he politely told me, "Goodnight, ma'am."

My lip quivered as I turned to go back upstairs. My addiction was getting the best of me. I headed back to the elevator not liking the feeling that I'd have to go all night without a smoke but also not liking the way the corridors had evolved into an eerie, spooky, antechamber that seemed longer than I remembered. A shiver traveled down my spine while I waited for the elevator. My senses acute; I heard the rattle of wheels on the tile floor down the hall beyond a turn. I stared into the emptiness, ready to see who or what was responsible for this noise. It stopped; then started again. Uneasiness lurked inside me.

Faintly, my eyes focused on the mysterious culprit. I sighed with relief. *It's a woman.* My overactive imagination calmed. Dressed all in white, she gradually got closer and stopped to unlock a door that was across from the elevator.

She took a look at me and with her Spanish accent, rolled each word spoken. "Sometimes they can be very slow at night. Maybe you should push the button one more time."

"Oh, okay." Retrieving a basket from the room, she locked the door and stood with me, ready to go up. Most likely in her forties, she had wavy brown hair and her olive complexion was smooth and flawless. She was not very tall. Grateful that I wasn't alone anymore, I couldn't hold back my smile. She smiled back at me as we listened for the elevator.

That's when she broke our silence. "You look so familiar to me."

"I've been coming here for almost two weeks. My husband had a brain aneurysm and up until today, has been in ICU." While chatting I noticed the shape of a cigarette box in her pocket. "You smoke?" I asked.

"Yes, do you need one?" She reached into her pocket.

"Yes. I mean, no, I have my own. That's what I came down here for, but the guard had the door locked, and I didn't want to get locked outside because it was dark, and..."

Taking me by the arm, she said, "Down there on the left, see that big door? Go, it will take you outside." I stared down the corridor and wanted to go but hesitated. I really didn't like what the hospital turned into at night.

"Do you want to go, too?" I asked, looking back at her.

She checked her watch and nodded her head affirmatively. "Si, I can take my break now." Gratefully, I let her lead me to a sliding glass door about twenty feet from the elevator. She stopped to buy a Pepsi from the vending machine and then pushed the handle on the door. A sign read EMPLOY-

EES ONLY. "We can have one out here."

A wire cage surrounded us, and large machinery hissed and hummed. I realized we were in the fenced area I had seen from the smoker's patio. A number of men speaking Spanish, ranging in all ages and sizes, were smoking and laughing with one another. We went to a bench to sit down. She told me her name was Gloria and we exchanged conversation. Gloria listened as I told her about Bill. Appearing surprised when I finished, Gloria spoke Spanish to the men, "Ey yos mio, her husband...we all heard he was a miracle. The pictures, Ey...the two of them...Deo Con es tu corozone." She continued in English, praising God for his mercy and told me how all the staff members had been aware of us due to the pictures on the wall in Bill's ICU room.

The men came closer, commenting to each other and then agreeing that I was the woman in the picture. Gloria revealed, "We all prayed for the two of you." I just gazed at her in amazement.

"I never dreamed that the pictures could have done this." I had difficulty finding the words to thank them. It didn't matter; my expression filled with gratitude seemed enough. I was blessed and enjoyed my short time with them. When I needed to return to Bill, Gloria and I hugged each other and promised to meet the next evening.

***

"He hasn't even moved." Annette whispered.

I thanked her, then thanked her again when I discovered pajama bottoms and a hospital shirt on my bed. She told me she had noticed I didn't have a bag and thought they might be needed. Annette instilled a feeling of security I hadn't felt in days. "How long will you be here?" I asked.

"Till eleven, sometimes I have a double shift." I thought that's a long time for a woman of her age. She continued, "I love my job. Here, I can give back." Her children and grandchildren were living in other states, and she started this job as a way to adjust, she explained. Having recently become a widow after many happy years with her husband, this was a way for her to tolerate being alone. She was enjoying telling me her little life stories, and I was happy to listen.

***

Annette made me remember my own grandmother. In 1962, after being in Florida for a few weeks, I asked, "Grandma, how do you know when you are in love? What does it feel like?" Waiting for an answer, I sat backwards in the kitchen chair, straddling the backrest, waiting for her response. "I think I love Billy," I added.

Grandma turned off the faucet and dried her hands on the little towel attached to her apron. Turning towards me, she pondered my question for a moment and then tenderly answered with her own words of wisdom. "When you don't mind picking up a man's dirty socks, that's when you know you are in love."

What an answer to give a twelve year old. Not understanding what she meant, I shrugged my shoulders.

"Grandma, dirty socks...?"

"Uh-huh, that's what I said." She smiled at me and told me, "One day you will understand what I mean."

I could hear Bill's breathing, and looked over at him. *It all makes sense. I don't mind at all. I shrugged my shoulders, just as I had done then.* "I love you, Bill."

Grandma, I get it.

Tired, I cleaned myself up and appreciated Annette's thoughtfulness. Washing out my undies, I hoped they would dry overnight. I finished tying the last two strands on my night shirt. "I hope they don't think I'm a patient here!" Annette smiled. I gave an unnoticed kiss to Bill, climbed into my bed and snuggled up.

"Good night, sleep well." Annette spoke softly.

"Good night, Annette.*" Good night, Grandma…*

***

Instinctively I yanked the pillow from under my head and put it over my face. The bright lights hurt my sleepy eyes. Doctors and nurses were talking as though no one in the room had been sleeping. I had to see what was going on. Rubbing my eyes, I sat up.

One of the attendants said, "Sorry didn't mean to disturb you." Bill was receiving meds and his sheets were being stripped. The whole place was lit up brightly and people were conversing. This scenario took place every hour on the hour. I'm going to go mad! All night long I heard them repeat, "Calm down, Mr. Faulkner. Don't pull that, Mr. Faulkner. Easy does it, Mr. Faulkner." Bill, whining and growling, persistently gave them a hard time. I wasn't sure what I should do, if I should help. I thought the night would never end.

In the wee hours of the morning, Bill had diarrhea in his bed. The stench covered him from his head to his toes and gagged anyone in close proximity. I was way too close… I had to find refuge in the hallway. I stood around while the nurses cleaned him up and gave a fleeting glance to the stranger in Annette's chair, *a new sitter?* In his knife-sharp creased pants and spit-shined shoes, he sat at attention, not moving a muscle. He looked like a retired drill sergeant ready to pounce on the first raw recruit who crossed his path. I held my arms over my flimsy night shirt, feeling somewhat self-conscious and murmured under my breath. "How can I do this?"

Chapter 20

Day after day I met new nurses, sitters, and diagnostic technicians. Bill's daily routine wasn't rocket science anymore. He was on a number of medications, but all his tubes and wires had been removed. Most of my time was spent attempting to soften his bristling quills. I knew Bill; the stranger inside him was not the man I married. He seemed to be struggling with a dark side I hadn't been aware of, and his temper was short; his kind nature stifled. The people we dealt with obviously wondered how I managed to stay so in love with this man. There were times I wondered the same thing. Could I love this changed man the way I had loved my cherished husband?

Bill had begun irritating me with a fairly common gesture of calling me 'dear.' Usually, couples who call one another 'dear' intend it to be sweet and flattering. Bill had warped the phrase into an annoying kind of ridicule towards me. When he was nagging, he'd say, 'Yes, dear,' and when he was being sarcastic he'd say, 'Yes, dear!' Bill could yell, whine, or state 'Yes, dear' and be so irritating, no matter how he spoke the phrase. In the beginning, he only said 'Yes, dear' to me; then graduated to whomever he might be speaking to. His verbal quills pierced many an innocent victim, and I found myself in the middle of a battle of confrontations. When he gave me a hard time, the nurses were ruthless. When Bill gave them a hard time, they went after blood.

I knew love had gotten us thus far. I struggled to keep calm and not let his attitude be discouraging. I needed to decode the secret map of his heart. Naptime, nighttime, hour after hour, I held tight to our strengths and focused on the great life we had known.

Wavering on a tight rope, I was barely keeping balance; yet I had to continue with devoted determination. I had to make my way to solid ground and find my lost treasure.

Two weeks of madness had passed, and professional medical assistance personnel were helping me with a plan for the future; our future. It was still too early to tell how much help Bill would need physically or mentally until he was satisfactorily healed. Medically, the surgeons were saying he was in pretty darn good shape. Everything they had done seemed to be holding, and no new problems were occurring. I was ecstatic to hear the news, and when they said he could be released from hospital care, I couldn't have felt more blessed.

Bill had always told me; sometimes I hear what I want. It's the way my brain works or just the 'ole stubborn genetics' I was born with. I was convinced released meant 'go home.'

A social worker came to his room to explain the plan. The woman went over the different tests, procedures, and medications Bill had needed in great detail. Listening carefully, I tried to absorb her explanations. Her file of paperwork was two inches thick with all his information.

I hadn't received any invoices as of yet and dreaded the costs involved. It'll take a lot of time to pay back all our debts, but it's worth every cent. Bill and I can sell something or I'll get a job. My mind drifted as I contemplated what my skills were. A high school graduate, I've taken care of a family, I've worked with my husband in our own business. I can paint really well. I've perfected that trade... I wonder if you have to have a license?

"Mrs. Faulkner, did you hear me?"

"I'm sorry. I was just thinking about all the bills, and what did you say?"

"As I was saying, there is a charity program through the hospital for the uninsured. Basically, the doctors and the hospital can 'write off' certain charges. As of today, your hospital bill and hospital expenses are going to be taken care of by this program. Your husband's bill, in laymen's terms, will be erased. The rehab has also accepted Mr. Faulkner as a patient, free of charge."

The figures were in the hundreds of thousands of dollars. I cried when she told me, almost feeling faint. What an unbelievable blessing! "Thank you, Jesus. Thank you all." Reaching out, I held the woman's hands. "Bill and I thank you...so much."

There was just one thing that was on my mind...I wanted to be released...we'd been in room 586 close to a week... we needed to go home... how could I phrase this? "Really, thank you so much. You have been so very kind. I will always praise God for all the help everyone here has given us, but..."

"That's what we are here for. You are very, very welcome, Mrs. Faulkner."

"There's one thing. I don't think the rehab program is going to be necessary." I didn't want to sound the least bit ungrateful. "I can take good care of Bill, and teach him, and certainly love him with all my heart. Besides, I really feel deeply indebted to all the doctors and the hospital and feel like I wouldn't want to take advantage. Dr. Grady said he was perfect! I think I should just take Bill home."

The woman stared at me with a confused expression. "This is something you will have to discuss with the doctor, Mrs. Faulkner." She waited in the visitor chair while I found Dr. Grady.

I pleaded with Dr. Grady, "Please, let us go home. It will be the best for him."

Listening to my reasoning, he asked, "Do you know what you'll be faced with?"

"I believe I can do this. I'll do art therapy, reading, games...and we have a pool for when he's ready for exercise."

With a quirky little grin and a shake of his head, he half-heartedly agreed to my plan, releasing Bill to my care. "Good luck, Mrs. Faulkner." He signed the papers and I was told we would be able to leave within the hour.

***

My sister Kathie offered to chauffeur us home that afternoon. During our ride I called Joyce on my cell phone. She was giving me what for, for not allowing Bill to go to free rehab. I reacted with, "You don't understand. He needs to get away from the doctors and nurses. They are making him crazy!"

"I certainly do to understand! He'd benefit from rehab." She was upset. She had given me her professional opinion, and I hadn't even considered she might be right. Joyce continued, "Northbay Hospital has an extraordinary rehabilitation program. It wouldn't be a comfort stay; he'd have to work hard. They have superb results."

"Well, we're on our way home..."

I was so relieved to be leaving the hospital that, while on the phone, I failed to pay attention to what was going on in the front seat. Kathie was scolding Bill and needed help. Bill was acting like a two-year-old. The buttons on the dashboard were his to be pushed, windows were opening and closing. He was distracting Kathie who was concentrating on the downtown traffic.

"I'm sorry, Kath. I should have been paying better attention." Kathie, with a death grip on the steering wheel, was sharing her attention between what Bill was doing and the road ahead. "Bill, keep your hands off the radio! Don't touch the heat. No! Not the rearview mirror." He was really getting out of hand. I repeated to my sister, "I'm sorry." I was relieved when I finally convinced him to recline in his seat and take a rest. That was until his hand inched toward the emergency brake between the two front seats.

"Settle down!" Kathie yelled. Previously an elementary school teacher, she employed the stern voice that teachers use to control an unruly class. I think it scared the bejeebers out of Bill. Voila! It was magical. He did what he was told.

Reaching over, he patted Kathie's knee, a gesture not well taken, "Yes, dear." Kathie didn't hesitate to indignantly push his hand away. Bill sulked. He turned away and for the rest of the ride home fidgeted with his seat belt.

All the way home, tension smoldered. The only words were whispered from Kathie, "Yes, dear, Humph."

***

We arrived at home. Our three children and all our grandchildren were there to greet Bill. Dave and Billy helped get Bill and all his stuff into the house. Bill was bossy and reluctant to use his walker. Rude and defiant and obviously tired, Bill seemed as though he had to show off. His ogre like persona bullied all of us. No one could tame him. I suggested, "Maybe it'd be best if we had a little quiet time."

Everyone gradually left; I'm sure with concern for our situation. Bill and I got ready for bed. Earlier, the kids had brought a bed downstairs so he wouldn't have to climb up and down the stairs. It was great having him home, sharing a bed, sleeping next to him. I slept like a log for the first time in two weeks. While I slept soundly, Bill made some trips to the bathroom during the night without asking for help. I recall him muttering; he had to crawl from the bathroom back to bed. I can only imagine if he had fallen, and to this day thank God for watching over him. I felt horrible. What on earth was I thinking? He wasn't ready to be home.

***

The following day he seemed lethargic and wouldn't respond to any prompting. Getting him to eat was extremely difficult; getting him to take his medications nearly impossible. By mid-afternoon I was scared. Bill was out of it. He couldn't (or wouldn't) drink or eat. He just laid in bed, curled up in a fetal position, listless.

In this half-asleep, half-awake state, Bill made a disastrous mess in the bed. I had watched the nurses during his stay at the hospital, and felt confident I could tackle the situation, but had no idea the job would be so difficult. He was lifeless and couldn't cooperate enough to roll over. Bill's six foot three, two hundred pound frame took more strength to move than I had. I cleaned his body, front, sides, and back. I placed newspapers under him in the process. When I finished, he rested on clean towels with fresh underwear and a clean sheet over him. I would have to wait for help to be able to change the soiled sheets. The whole process took the good part of an hour. Only then did I break down and cry.

I wiped away my tears; I struggled to compose myself. The doorbell was ringing, and I remembered that outside resources for rehab had been scheduled. A young man arrived to start Bill's therapy. He was surprised at Bill's motionless body. We stared at Bill curled up in the bed, weak, and confused. Returning to the hospital seemed to be my only choice. I had been so stubborn about bringing him home in the first place. The young man and I agreed; he had come home too soon. Totally discouraged, I prayed, "Oh, please God, help me fix this."

I made the call to 911 and the ambulance came. An hour later, Bill was back in room 586 at the hospital since he was not a patient at the rehab. I rode to Clearwater grimacing. Northbay Hospital in New Port Richey was only four miles from our home; Morton Plant Hospital, thirty-five. Social workers came and went. No one could get back our lost opportunity. A bed at rehab was out of the question. The bed had already been assigned to another patient. Frustrated and exhausted, I prayed and begged: "Lord, help me out." *Please forgive me for being so thickheaded...*

***

I shared the room at the hospital with Bill for what seemed like an eternity. I couldn't see an end to this horrible nightmare coming soon. He improved slightly; yet I could see that he would need therapy and rehabilitation with each passing day. For the first time in my life, I doubted if God was hearing my prayers. I felt as though I had been sentenced to imprisonment, and the hospital room was my jail cell. Bill's attitude left me unsettled in our relationship. He treated me miserably, and I was left with very little to give. The more anyone helped him, the more he demanded. Bill acted as if the world owed him, and he didn't care who he upset on his journey.

"Good morning, Mr. Faulkner. Let's get you cleaned up and ready for breakfast."

"No."

"I think you might want to shave those whiskers and brush your teeth."

"No!"

The nurse pushed the button to raise Bill's bed. "It's a lovely morning, sir. Let's get a fresh gown on you, and you can take a walk in the hallway."

"No." He looked at me. "Tell her to get out of here!" By now I had sat up in my little bed. I buttoned my lip as she continued with her job. I could see she probably thought her job stunk when it came to times like this. Bill grabbed her arm. "Do you want to help? Let's get married and get out of here!"

"I don't think so, Mr. Faulkner. I see you already have a beautiful wife."

He dropped her arm and glared at me. "She doesn't matter!"

Chapter 21

Shattered, I laid back down, agonizing about Bill and this wretched life. I curled up on my cot and closed my eyes. I couldn't listen to his nonsense anymore. I wondered how his brain was working and if it would be stuck like this forever. So different, my husband was a stranger.

When the nurse left the room, I expected tears would have streamed from my eyes; I felt so hopeless. But instead of tears, a flood of emptiness flushed through my broken heart. I was in a lonely place without Bill. I was so hurt; yet I couldn't vent to him; he didn't understand. My inner light flickered. I had no tears, no painful sighs; just a vacant feeling.

The visitor chair slid on the floor, startling me. A woman was sitting in the far corner of the room. Had this lady been here long? Another sitter, she took her position in our room. I peeked as I squinted. My eyes were slit enough to see her, but I hoped she would think I was still sleeping. I was in no mood for having a stranger in our room, speculating on our every move. I understood the sitter's purpose but still felt my privacy was being invaded.

The woman was well groomed, black, probably my age. Her wavy dark brown hair was reminiscent of the women in the 1940's: contoured around her face with a two finger wave over her right brow. Her hair was shiny and sleek, and she looked very attractive. She wore a dark blue summer dress with tiny little flowers on it. With capped sleeves, it too looked like the 40's. I wondered where she found it in today's market. A pleasant scent drifted towards me, fresh air and honeysuckle coming to mind. All and all, she had accomplished a look of sweet Southern charm with a taste of finery, a dash of sexy.

I shut my eyes to stop looking at her. I felt like a henhouse hag and probably smelled like one, too. My hair needed washing, and I hadn't had a real shower in at least three days.

I heard the pages turn as she read her book and knew she wasn't going to go away any time soon. When I couldn't hold my morning bathroom call a minute longer, I crept past her without a word. Some clean towels were piled on the sink. I began soaping every inch of my body. *This is a little better.* I brushed my teeth and braided my hair. I was glad I had brought clean clothes to put on this time. *Thank God, for something...* My spirits climbed a little as I smelled my skin after dabbing on my own cologne.

This definitely was an improvement, but I still wasn't feeling bright and shiny enough to talk when I came out of the bathroom. I needed coffee. Walking past her again, I left her to her sitter job. I didn't have a need to socialize. Bill had already forgotten what an ass he had been, and my Shalimar seemed to spark a subtle memory. The glow quickly faded. Bill was looking for breakfast. I spoke to him long enough to find out what he wanted and ordered down. The room offered a menu, and this worked out fairly well with the unorthodox way he ate his meals. It was like a restaurant; full service lunch, dinner or breakfast anytime between six A.M. and nine P.M. *In the Navy, Bill worked night shifts. I never knew if it was breakfast or dinner that would delight his pallet.* I ordered his meal, myself some coffee, and didn't give it another thought. I waited around until his breakfast came and, after setting it up for him, took my coffee and headed for the ground floor. *Humph...he can eat alone!*

My friend Mark was sitting at our table when I joined him. "Hey Mark, how ya doing? I haven't seen you in a couple days."

"I've been here. Where were you?"

I shared all my woes. He shared his miserable life with me as well, and we drank coffee and smoked cigarettes for about an hour. I told him about Gloria and Annette and my short trip back home. He had gone through hell himself and, to top it off, thought I had left without saying goodbye.

Men! I didn't try to make any excuses. "When we leave, I'll let you know next time. I promise, okay? But right now I've got to go. I have to check on Bill."

"My wife is still on the fifth floor. I'll walk you up."

"Okay, thank you."

I returned to the room while Bill was napping. The sitter was still reading her book. I waited for awhile before introducing myself. "My name's Valerie." I glanced over to Bill. "He's my husband."

"Good morning, Valerie. You can call me Rose." Her voice was as nice sounding as her appearance, and her Southern accent made me think of drinking ice cold lemonade while nibbling on tea cookies. Rose wore a delicate little cross around her neck. She had a gift for conversation, and the longer we talked, the better it got. She was a Christian who praised the Lord with such graciousness whenever she had the chance. We found we had so much in common as we spoke about our families and children and grandchildren. Rose was born the same year I was.

She had some good times in her life and told me all about them, but she also had more than her share of rough times. My jaw dropped when she said she was married four times. One of her daughters and two grandchildren lived with her in St. Petersburg. She endured things I had never had to struggle with, and yet she had a smile and a strength that surrounded her. The spirit she possessed she shared, glowing inside and out. Rose was a ray of sunshine, sending a sparkle into my dull veneer. I wanted to be near her; she reflected a peace that

I needed and a calm that rolled atop the waves. Rose's guiding principle for getting along in life was not to fret; it never solved anything. "You got to put your worries in God's hands, Val."

As the afternoon flew by, I thought about what she said. We chatted about work and shopping and not enough money but, worse than that, not enough time. We laughed; I thought I had forgotten how. We raised our hands together as we chimed in 'Hallelujahs,' discovering a bond that felt like no other. I related to Rose like I had known her forever. This stranger was so much like me; it was uncanny.

She agreed; we were like old friends; everlasting friends who had run into each other after years gone by. I told her, "I think God has sent you so I'd have someone to talk and laugh with. Thank you, Rose. I needed you today."

"Oh, no there's no doubt at all in my mind. God sent *you* so *I* would have someone to talk and laugh with! God bless you, Val." When her workday ended, we hugged each other. Both knew we met not by chance but because of our Father in heaven.

Bill hadn't changed much that day, but I did. Rose helped me just by being there. The day went by so fast, and I knew I had to be strong like Rose to get through the days ahead.

Of course, that theory wasn't holding up as well as I hoped. When each sitter arrived, I wished for a book of safety instructions. I repeated that Bill needed help if he wanted to leave his bed and that the sign on his door confirmed he was a fall risk. Not worrying was a tough job, and then I'd think about Rose. Repeatedly I told myself, "Put it in God's hands."

Shauna was about eighteen and very cute and came in to sit after Rose. Bill was acting up. I had to apologize to this poor girl and told her that my husband wasn't always such a letch and if he gave her a hard time, to call for help. Bill had dinner and I warily left him with this girl. "I'll only be about fifteen minutes. My cell number is on the chalkboard. Thank you… I won't be long."

Bill was aggravating me. Any and all past insecurities I harbored were boiling over inside of me. I needed a break. Disheartened, I couldn't see him this way. I had lost count of how many times he asked Shauna to marry him. I went downstairs to cool off and get away. Keeping my word, I returned quickly.

Shauna was watching the maintenance man mop up the floor. "I'm so sorry. Your husband insisted I help him to the bathroom."

I stared at the man and her. "What happened?"

Hearing my question, a nurse entered,. "He fell. Shauna didn't get assistance and he went down, the tray followed. His plastic urinal went, too!" Bill's expression showed no remorse as the nurse scolded, "You're a lucky man, Mr. Faulkner!"

Shauna had tears in her eyes. I had to let her know how I felt about this whole scenario. "Shauna, I trusted you! I needed a break and should have been able to go…damn."

I could feel my heart throbbing as I tried to calm myself. Anyone could see she was beyond herself, and gradually I reconsidered my indignant attitude and found pity on the young girl.

"I'm not mad. Everybody makes a mistake once and a while. Bill can be very convincing." I paused to catch my breath, "Just let this be a lesson for the future. Thank God he didn't get hurt."

"Thank you."

"I'm not blaming you. I understand…"

For the rest of the evening I hung out and babysat. I was tired but couldn't sleep. Hospital life was making me restless.

My mind was in overdrive, and I couldn't find any solutions for this mind- boggling puzzle. At about eleven P.M. Shauna left and a short, stocky man made himself at home in our room. I was sitting in the dark with my box of tissues; the only light filtering into the room was from the hall. Bill was sleeping while I watched TV, off and on.

"Good evening, my name is Luis." He spoke English very well but had a slight accent. He wore a suit.

I cleared my throat, "Valerie."

"Is he your husband?"

"Yes...his name is Bill."

"It's very nice to meet you, Valerie and Bill." He could see Bill was sleeping and moved his chair closer to mine. "I don't want to disturb your husband." Sniffling, I grabbed a fresh tissue and wiped my nose. I really wasn't in the mood to talk to Luis. I stared at the TV. "So... why are you so sad?"

"Oh, I'm not. I'm just tired."

"You have been through a lot?"

I looked at him, sighing, "Yes, I have." I knew I couldn't control my tears with him asking all these questions. If I just kept watching the TV, he would get the hint and leave me alone. I'd had enough of sitters for one day.

"Tell me. What happened?"

"It's a long story. I've also had a long day." I heard Bill making gurgling noises and got up to check him. When I sat back down, Luis was waiting for me to go on. I was reluctant to speak, but his prodding continued. I gave in, telling him a condensed version. Luis listened. "And that's pretty much all of it. I really didn't want to rehash all this!"

"Don't yell." Luis smugly gave me a look.

With a loud whisper I scolded, "I wasn't!"

"Why are you worrying? You should be counting your blessings and giving him a little slack. Your husband is obviously improving."

"I'm not. Well, I am. What do you mean 'why am I worrying?'" *Luis was so annoying. How could he ever imagine what I had been through? Why was he bothering me like this?* "Give Bill some slack?" *Uh, you sound like a male chauvinist.*

"Yes!"

Blowing my nose, I again stared at the television. Luis was relentless. I didn't even want to listen to him; he was such a jerk.

"God has a plan for each of us. Our life is in his hands." He began to tell me his story. His wife had died years ago and most of his children were gone now, too. My heart sank as he continued. I loathed the fact that he was able to keep my attention. I watched him as I listened.

He had come to America when he was a young boy, barely a teenager. A small boat from Cuba brought him here, along with a few other surviving family members. He witnessed the death of many people, mostly his relatives. Journeying to America took many days as he sat amongst the dead or dying. My hand cupped my mouth as I felt his pain. I wished I could take back all the sarcasm that had drifted through my mind.

Finishing his story on a happier note, Luis told me that one of his favorite parts of life was being a clown. He still had gigs he worked and loved making people happy.

"A clown, really?" Giggling, I pictured this man all dressed up like a clown. "What kind of clown? How do you dress up?"

"Like Emmett Kelly. Do you remember him?"

I stopped giggling and looked into Luis' eyes. "Yes, I do.

He's the only clown who never seemed creepy. He was just…
sad…"

Just like Emmett Kelly, I could see a tear on his cheek.

Luis held his hand out to me, acting as though he wanted
to say something very important. "Closer, give me your
hand." Putting my hand in his, he went on. "You always have
to try and keep God close to your heart. Life is but a journey
to heaven. Believe in the power of prayer. God listens to us
when we pray to Him; He hears us. He will guide us in a way
any father would with his child; leading us, holding our hand
all the way."

As he gently held my hand, I could see that his faith had
brought him through many a difficult time. A feeling of seren-
ity came over me as I realized that Luis was so absolutely
right. After leading us in a prayer, he said goodnight.

I closed the curtain and lay down in my little bed. *I need
to let God take care of Bill. He needs to be able to heal and
find his own way. God, hold his hand. God, please hold mine
too.*

Chapter 22

Eighteen days had passed, and Bill seemed encased in a hardened shell. I couldn't find a miraculous nutcracker in my proverbial tool pouch. I had been holding on to a live wire, wondering, could my own troubleshooting skills eradicate the sparks?

All the people I met were like messengers from above, certainly helping in my moments of need, but Andy was different. As the young man entered our room, I watched him shuffle across the floor.

"Helwo. My name is Andy." He plopped in one of the visitor chairs. "I'm gonna read this book today. It's my favorite book in the whole world. I been reading it for *awong* time, but today I think I'll finish it." I gazed at him, knowing there was definitely something wrong. Bill was awake and murmured something about being a quart low. Knowing what he meant, I hushed him for being rude.

Andy held his book about six inches from his face. He was about six feet tall, and his head was larger than normal, even for his size. His jeans were high at his waste, held tight with a brown belt displaying an ornamental cowboy buckle. His oversized socks draped over the top of his sneakers, leaving his ankles showing. His shoes were barely tied. He sat reading his page for a good fifteen minutes, then paused. "I should have brought another book. When I finish this, I won't have one to read." He laughed a little. "Oh, well. I can just read this one again."

To a nurse in the hallway, I said, "I'd like to go downstairs. A man named Andy is in my husband's room."

Acknowledging me, the nurse said, "Okay."

"Do you think Andy will be all right with Bill?"

"Yes."

"Do you know Andy?"

"Yes, they'll be fine." She started to walk away and turned back, "He's worked here for a number of months. He does a very good job." I didn't say anything and headed for the elevator. Luis' memory and Rose's words played games in my mind.

Yeah, don't worry...easier said than done!

When I returned, a couple of new doctors were reading the charts outside of Bill's room. They were glad to find me; they needed permission for administering drugs. Having never had seen them, I asked all the pertinent questions. They promised the meds would keep Bill calmer and were imperative to his health. Calmer sounded good.

"Okay. I guess so." I signed the paper.

It was lunch time and I trekked down to the cafeteria. Like a lightning bolt, I remembered what the little nurse had said when we had moved to room 586. *Stay away from...*

"Shit!" I ran back to the nurse's station, leaving my lunch on the table. "Some doctors were here before. What kind of doctors were they?"

"They are from the seventh floor, Mrs. Faulkner, Psychiatrics."

"I don't want Bill to take any meds from them. I've changed my mind."

"I'm sorry. The orders have been charted."

"Well, I want you to remove those orders! I don't want

Bill taking anything from those doctors."

Pulling out the files, she told me she would see what could be done. "It may take a couple hours, but I'll let you know." I returned to the room to guard against evil and found Andy still reading, Bill awake. What an odd couple they made; one meek and mild, the other willful and harsh. Not a word was spoken until a nurse showed up to give Bill his pills. I made a point to find out what each pill was and what it was for.

"This one is for seizures, this for blood pressure, this, too, is for B.P. and this is another type for seizures, and the last one for stool softening." She looked Bill in the eyes, having cleaned him up just hours before. "I don't think you need these, do you, Mr. Faulkner?" She smirked as I answered for him.

"No! What else are you giving him?"

"This is just a vitamin. I'll make a note about the stool softener."

I watched Bill swallow. "And no calmatives, right?"

"That's right. Oh, his paperwork was updated. It says only if Mrs. Faulkner is asked first."

"Thank you. I guess that means they've taken them off. I don't have to worry that you're going to slip one in?"

"Don't worry. He won't be given any without your permission."

"Thank you."

Andy, observing our conversation, asked me, "What happened to Bill?" I wasn't sure how to explain to him what had happened so just told it like it was.

"Bill had a ruptured brain aneurysm."

"Oh. Can he walk?"

"He's getting there. It will be a little while before he's perfect."

"Can he read?"

I didn't know. "I think so."

With that, Bill rolled over and murmured under his breath, "Can I walk…"

"Can he talk?"

"Yes, but I think he's tired now, Andy."

"God will take care of him. God took care of me. I couldn't walk. I couldn't read. I love to read! I didn't have what he had. I had a *blain bleed.*" I felt a lump in my throat. I realized Andy didn't know the medical terminology. He smiled, "And now I have a job, and… I'm… perfect."

Chapter 23

I made it through another few days but couldn't find a way to communicate with Bill. His actions were stronger than words, and my heart ached, my own blood pressure skyrocketing. I knew I couldn't stand for this abuse any longer. I considered what Luis had said. *Okay, I'll give him some slack!*

I asked one of the nurses to take my blood pressure, and, for me 140/90 was very high. Dr. Grady recommended I go home and take a break. I wasn't exactly persuaded. He momentarily placed his arm on my shoulder and, shedding his stern business façade, promised, "Bill will be fine. Everything will be better after a good night's rest". He almost seemed to understand my bewilderment. Abruptly changing back to his old self, he repeated in a sterner, more typical voice, "Go. He'll be fine."

***

Kathie and Dave picked me up about eight P.M. The ride was quiet. In the back seat I slouched and stared out the window, watching as the light poles blinked by. Feeling defeated, I tried to convince myself that my reason for leaving was the pounding headache from my elevated blood pressure. In reality, I had to get away from Bill. My thoughts searched for anything to relieve my guilt. *Did I do the right thing?* Our lives were bound tighter than that. I was only stretching the rope. In my own defense, I concluded: it didn't seem to bother Bill at all when I told him I was leaving.

I called as soon as I arrived at home. "I'm just checking

in. Hello, Bill?" He wasn't holding the phone correctly. I could hear him mumbling into the phone. "Honey, turn it around; you have the phone up side down!" I yelled and told him again, "Turn the phone around!" Bill didn't. He didn't speak. All I heard was his breathing. He had fallen asleep. It took me forever to get back through to the hospital to tell a nurse to help him with his phone. I eventually spoke to him for about two minutes, finishing with my goodbyes. "I love you... Goodnight." I was glad when he put the nurse back on. "He'll be all right?"

The nurse on duty answered, "He'll be fine. Rest up. I'll check periodically to make sure his phone is on the receiver in case you want to call again."

"Thank you."

"You're welcome, Mrs. Faulkner, Goodnight."

***

It was close to midnight. I sat on the edge of my bed. My towel was still wrapped around me; the shower had cleansed my tired out bones. It was nice to feel my hairless legs, and it felt good to have my hair washed. Pulling down the covers, I propped up the pillows. Our queen-sized bed was certainly pleasant after my little cot. Tylenol had stopped my pounding headache, but I just couldn't stop reviewing everything that had been happening. I wished my brain would slow down and relax. I was glad I caught up with Mark to tell him I was going home. He said he was leaving, too. His wife was being transferred to a nursing home. *Poor Mark, I feel so bad for him. He's been a good friend. I wonder what will happen to him now. At least he gave me his phone number. I'll have to call him in a couple days.* Over and over, like old movie reruns, I couldn't turn my thoughts off. The days and nights, sitters, nurses, doctors. "God, give me some peace, please?"

It was late and I decided to read 'Quiet Moments with

God, for Couples', the book that Bill had given me for Christmas. We had been reading the stories to each other for the past few months before this all happened. I hoped a diversion would help me to calm down. Setting up my 'Pillow Bill,' I began. "Bill? Here's the bookmark from the last time. Now just lay there and listen; I'll read to you."

Each story had a lesson. I went through about five pages, reading out loud to my imaginary hubby. I looked at the heap of pillows on Bill's side of the bed and adjusted the sheet. "I wish you could really hear these. Hmm, maybe you can. You know, this was probably for the best. Absence makes the heart grow fonder, *Right?"*

After reading a few more, I stopped, looked at the heap of fluff, folded my hands and lay in the quiet room, talking to God. "Please, Lord. I'll do anything, just help me find him. Bill has never been this way! He was a good man. He was a good husband. Please help him. Help us."

I was feeling like such a nag. "Sorry God." I got up and brought back a bottle of water and plopped back in to bed. Billy was still out and the house seemed big and very quiet. Jake's gentle snoring was only a small comfort. "Okay, one last story before I go to sleep. Ready?" I patted 'Pillow Bill' and started. The tale was about grapes and vines and trees, a vague analogy not making much sense. When I finished, I thought, *I don't get it.* Looking at my fluffed up husband, I asked, "Should I try that again? Or are you sleeping?" Since there were no objections, I read the short story over and over. After the fourth try, it all came together.

It's how we all need one another. One is dependent on the other to survive. "I think I get it..." I lifted my eyes from the book and stared out into my desolate room.

I attempted to go through a couple more stories on my own and read silently. The words written were merely streaks of black; I couldn't concentrate on what they were telling.

Placing the book down, I realized I'd never had known such loneliness in my whole life. Certainly I could go through the actions of comforting myself; I could fool myself with my pillow Bill....but in reality I was kidding only me. Sobbing, I felt cloaked in misery.

Lonely and desperate, I choked on my tears and sniffles, and I breathlessly cried out to our Lord. I had too many questions I couldn't answer, and I prayed. "God.... I need You. I have loved this man for all my life. I don't know what to do. I wish I were strong but I need him, I miss him.... I know I can't turn back the clock, but I wish you would help me find my way on this wretched, frightening path. Tell me how I can go on."

"Tell the stories."

I heard those words.... I was shocked and sat still; curiously I listened. I could hear my heart beating, no other sound. Hesitantly I spoke in slightly more than a whisper, "What did you say?"

There was no thunder....no flashes of light, just a gentle voice that told me directly and to the point; once more, I heard the words spoken, "Tell the stories."

Repeating what I heard and answering, I still wasn't sure even yet that I had heard this right, "Tell the stories? What stories?"

I rubbed my eyes; I gazed around the bedroom. I wasn't dreaming; I hadn't been asleep. Jake was still in his bed. I was alone, yet felt a presence.

I asked once more, "Tell what stories? I don't know how to tell stories."

I heard nothing more but suddenly... I understood the meaning of the words. My mind was flooded with the night at Bob Evans, Bill's ability to survive, the unbelievable Jeep ride. I remembered the different sitters God had brought to comfort me and restore my faith. His presence was there when Gloria appeared in the darkened hallway the woman who prayed with co-workers because of the pictures on the ICU wall.

I knew at that moment, my purpose... what ever happened, I must tell the stories of all the miracles.

I spoke up, "I will, but I need Bill's help. I can't do this alone!" I searched for examples to elaborate my plea, "He's read lots of books and can help me. We could do this together." Once more I waited, seeking for even a whisper, hoping I'd hear back from the voice.

Nothing more; quietness filled the room leaving me to just sit in awe and think about those words. A feeling of peace surrounded me, and although a tad unsure, I knew what I must do. Without further hesitation, I came up with the only response I could think of.

"I'll tell the stories… I promise."

***

The next morning I rolled out of bed, ready to make some changes in my life. I thought about the night before but hastened to take care of today. My first and foremost thought was to do whatever it took to stay away from the hospital. I didn't want to go back. I needed to get Bill out. I decided to call the rehab center at Northbay Hospital in New Port Richey. In all bureaucracies there are channels, and the medical advisor at Morton Plant was not having any luck. I had some time to make an attempt on my own. Someone had told me of a Mrs. Bell, who was in charge of admitting.

I hoped if I spoke to Mrs. Bell personally, she'd reconsider Bill. I needed to tell her how my husband desperately needed rehab and that I was sorry for letting his chances go. After I dialed, I knew I couldn't blow my chances this time and nervously listened to the rings.

The dreaded voicemail politely asked me to leave a message. I hated leaving a message but did and then waited impatiently for the call back. Hours passed. I found myself making up excuses for Mrs. Bell.

First, I figured she must be in an extremely important meeting. Then noon came and I told myself she must take lunch – half an hour? Oh, no, she's too important. She must take an hour lunch. Possibly, executives get an hour and a half? Three hours passed; she finally returned my call.

Introducing myself, I told her of my dilemma. I practically begged. She was positive. "There aren't any beds available."

I dropped names, hoping that would work. I was desperate. I told her my sister Joyce worked as an ER nurse at Northbay for many years. "My sister told me that your rehab is the very best." We chatted politely, but I could tell by her tone of voice: our conversation was not going to get Bill the bed he needed.

Our talk was ending. I felt defeat was inevitable when she suddenly remarked, "What's your sister's full name?"

"Joyce Wagner."

"Oh, sorry, I can't say that I know her." She paused for a second then surprised me with a very silly question. "Has Joyce ever shopped Entenmann's?"

What's that? Is this a trick question? Clothing... Shoes... Makeovers, what's Entenmann's? "Oh... do you mean the bakery?"

"Yes."

"Uh, I don't know."

She explained that she had met a wonderful woman while shopping at Entenmann's. Mrs. Bell began telling me about the lady, a charter boat captain.

***

Joyce was totally in love with her exciting new career. She had been a nurse for over twenty years, and, although she loved nursing, after so long she suffered from a bit of burnout. Her boat was her baby. Anyone could see in her eyes she was ecstatic and rejuvenated with an excitement like never before. Hardly a sentence was muttered without a connection to her new profession. Her fish stories were better than any old salt, and like all great fisherman, she would hook you and reel you in.

***

"That's my sister!" After I described her, Mrs. Bell agreed Joyce was the same woman she met at Entenmann's Bakery.

In a more caring and tolerant voice, she told me she would have to talk to her floor supervisors. She promised to call me back. While I waited for her call, I thought about all of this. The chance meeting between her and my sister, according to Mrs. Bell, had happened weeks before. My sister's presence made our family real. Joyce was human; we were her family. Mrs. Bell gave me good news a half hour later. She informed me when the paperwork was complete, I could move Bill.

I called my sister to tell her Bill was going to rehab. She was happy but let me know, "You two are very lucky. Usually interfering with the system gets you nowhere." She acted like a big sis. I was thinking about how she met Mrs. Bell.

"How long have you shopped at Entenmann's? You never mentioned it."

"I don't," was her reply.

"Then, how...? This is strange. I'm confused."

"I went because Mom asked if I would stop for her. I stopped in on my way home from visiting you and Bill at the hospital."

Chapter 24

On Saturday I asked Stacie if she wanted to ride down to Morton Plant with me. I have to admit I probably didn't have a lot of desperation in my voice, and she gave me the perfect excuse; "Dad can wait another day. You have to take care of yourself, Mom." In her opinion, I needed another day to rest; after all I hadn't had a day off in almost three weeks. "Go tomorrow."

I felt it my duty to be with Bill; I had spent thirty-seven years being a dutiful wife. I hadn't told the kids about Bill's attitude towards me and her concern gave me the escape I had actually wanted. After weighing out the pros and cons, I decided to be selfish... Give Bill one more day to miss me.

I stayed home and distracted myself with house cleaning and laundry. It was nice to be home, and I allowed myself a stress free day to calm my disgruntled attitude. During my mindless tasks I wondered about Bill. I would have thought by now he'd be jumping for joy to be alive. I prayed through out the day and asked God to help him realize how blessed he was. I prayed for myself that I might understand and not be discouraged. "Thank you God at least it looks like he'll be going to rehab."

By Sunday morning I felt like a new person, ready to deal with my challenges head on. I clicked off the radio when *'Rise-Up'* ended at ten o'clock and grabbed the phone. I wanted to let Bill know I'd be leaving soon. He didn't answer. I tried the hospital number, catching up with his room nurse.

"I was just trying to call you Mrs. Faulkner. We're getting ready to transport your husband to Northbay Rehab Center."

I couldn't believe my ears. "He's getting out of the hospital today?"

"Yes."

"It's Sunday! Why didn't anyone tell me?" *Did I hear her correctly?* "Did a Mrs. Bell arrange this, already?"

"I really don't know about that. He's going downstairs as we speak."

"Really today, isn't this Memorial Day weekend?" I was talking a mile a minute.

The nurse interrupted me, "Yes, Mrs. Faulkner. And uh, yes, he's leaving here today." She began perfecting her enunciation. "I called your house…, but the line was busy. He'll arrive in New Port Richey in about two hours."

I couldn't contain myself. I wanted to jump up and down. "Don't mind me, I'm just so surprised. Please tell him I'll meet him there. I'll go early. It's only five minutes away…thank you so much for calling."

She started to laugh, "I think you called here, but okay, Mrs. Faulkner. I'll tell him."

Hanging up the phone, I hopped around the kitchen. Jake flounced at my feet, and we danced in a circle. I screamed, "Billy, Dad's going to rehab! *Thank you God…*Will you call Stacie and Shaye and tell them while I get ready?"

Billy came running downstairs, "Today?" One look at me answered his question. "Yeah, I'll call them. This is great!"

*****

I left the house knowing I'd be early. At the nurses' station a pleasant young woman informed me the trans-port was on its way. This was the first time I had seen the rehab, and I sat down to wait. An old computer filled a corner, and bright colorful pictures were scattered about the walls. I could hardly believe Bill was on his way to New Port Richey and that we were having another wonderful blessing. As I sat waiting I closed my eyes and thanked God. I couldn't wait to see Bill. I wanted this to be the beginning of our future....and I was ready to help him, to be the best he could be.

Suddenly my cell phone rang. "Valerie?" The phone crackled, and I couldn't make out the words being said.

"I can't hear you; you're breaking up. Hold on, let me walk outside. Is that better? Hello?"

"Yes. Hi, Valerie I'm the nurse you talked to earlier. Your husband left his wedding band here. We found it when we were changing the sheets. Do you want to come and get it?"

My mind flashed into an array of thoughts, and I couldn't speak. *What? We had promised each other to always wear our rings. He never took his ring off.*

"Valerie? Can you pick it up? We'll hold it at the nurses' station. I'll put it in an envelope for you. Are you there?"

I felt as though the breath had been sucked out of me, and I couldn't talk in a normal tone, just a whimper, "I'm at Northbay, waiting for my husband." My heart was filled with disbelief. "Maybe my daughter can come and get it...I'll find out if she can. Her name is Shaye."

"Okay, I'll put her name down as a second pick-up person."

"All right..." I put the phone on my belt loop and leaned against the concrete wall. *Why would he take his ring off? Was he finished with me? Had he tried to give it away? Was his mind so changed, indifferent, altered by the brain aneurysm?* I walked back inside and sat down in one of the waiting

183

chairs. With all my doubts, the memory I had of our thirtieth anniversary, seven years before, came to mind.

***

Bill and I vowed to do something special. We talked about going on a vacation or maybe getting something new for the house. We considered dinner and a show, or maybe going dancing... we loved to dance. We talked about what we would do when we came home...he and I loved talking about that. The months were flying by, and we hadn't had a chance to actually finalize any of our plans.

I remember it was the end of April and we were working. "Val, would you like to get new rings?"

I looked at my ring finger. Bill knew I had been worried about my rings. "The reason I haven't been wearing one is because I don't want to lose my diamond. God, I'd die if I lost it on a job. This work is too hard for frills."

Bill looked at me, "We could get white gold bands, no frills."

I thought about it and got so excited. "We'd match? I'd love that!"

The jeweler helped us pick out the perfect wedding bands. "Would you like them engraved?"

Both Bill and I shrugged. Stumped, we discussed back and forth what we might like, engraved inside our rings forever; together we agreed.

Bill spoke, "Mr. Jeweler, we want three numbers, roman numerals: III, II, I."

I spoke up, "And our wedding date, 5-11-68."

"And 'Val and Bill'...do you think you can fit it in?" Bill waited for the man to answer.

"Yes. Give me one week and you can pick them up." We walked out holding hands, swinging our arms.

We remembered when we got married the minister told us at the rehearsal that he was glad we were having a double ring ceremony. He explained that a ring... a circle is but a symbol; but we should always wear them to remind us what the symbol stands for. A life in marriage, no beginning... no end... perpetual... forever; we had always worn them.

We both were so excited; we couldn't wait for the day to come. On our anniversary, we celebrated our thirty years with the most beautiful matching rings. The roman numerals are like our hand squeezes. "I love you. Mean it? Yes...."

Then why did he take it off?

***

After awhile the transport van pulled up. The driver assisted Bill into a wheelchair. I stood watching their approach from inside. The automatic doors opened, and Bill was wheeled through. I could see he seemed confused and lost. His body looked frail; his hair uncombed lying flatter on one side. He wore his own clothes, but they draped over his body like they were two sizes too big. He still wore hospital slippers. It made my heart ache to see him like this; he looked so out of it.

He didn't see me right away. Hurting and confused, I certainly wasn't going to make a big deal of the ring thing right then, but I could hardly speak. *What had happened to him?* My heartstrings were shredding... I bit my lip, and I stood in front of him.

"Bill...? Hi..." He looked up and, taking notice of me, his beautiful blue eyes gazed into mine. His smile conveyed a happiness that I'd known and remembered for so long. *There had to be something, a reason; I just wasn't getting it.*

Reaching to his side, he secured the brake on the wheelchair and struggled to stand. The attendant didn't try to stop him. I held out my hand, but he wanted to do this on his own.

Standing tall, he pulled up his loose jeans, fixed his shirt, and held his arms out. He shuffled two steps and then wrapped his arms around me. He kissed the top of my head and drew my face close to his. I'm sure he could see the tears around my eyes; they were in his, too. Kissing my lips, he held his face inches from mine, staring at my face. His smile broadened, and he pulled me closer. He whispered in my ear, "You feel so good."

I looked up at him, "Bill...you do, too." Holding each other, we kissed once more, memories flooded my head. I felt as though we were both searching for the unforgettable love we had known so well. Yet, something seemed strange... unclear... I could feel a difference... I couldn't pin point what, but it was like a negative energy coming between us.

We held tight until his legs got wobbly, and he had to sit back down. As the nurse pushed his wheelchair, we strolled to his room; Bill wanted to hold my hand.

While helping him get settled in, the nurse handed me a paper: 'Visitor Instruction Sheet.' Skimming over it, I could see the no nonsense approach that Joyce had told me about was indeed a fact. "Sounds like boot camp."

I wasn't actually kidding, but she took it that way and chuckled, "Maybe just a little."

"Visiting hours end at six?"

"Yes, they do. You can stay a tad longer since it's his first day."

"Thank you. I think my daughter will be here in about ten minutes or so; will that be all right?"

"That will be fine." She briefly explained a little about the rehabilitation program and then turned to leave. "I'll be back in a few minutes with your meds, Mr. Faulkner."

When she left the room, Bill grabbed my hand again and held tight. I asked, "Bill, did you miss me?"

"Yes. I did."

I leaned down to kiss his hand. He brought my hand up to his lips and kissed mine. "I missed you too, honey. I needed to go home. I'm sorry."

"It's okay. I knew you'd come back."

I smirked and nudged him. "Were you sure about that?"

Bill kept staring at me. First, he didn't answer, and then he smiled. "Well, pretty sure." Patting his hand on the bed, he motioned for me to sit beside him. "Come here, you."

As I sat down, Shaye arrived, "Hi, Dad!" She walked in and gave us both a hug and a kiss. She handed me Bill's ring. "So Dad, how are you doing?"

Bill answered, "A little tired. It was a long ride."

I held his wedding band in the palm of my hand. "Shaye just went down to Morton Plant to pick up your ring. Did you know you lost this?" My face can't hide emotion very well. He could see in my expression that I was upset.

Bill looked at his hand to check out his ring finger and gasped. "Shit! How'd that happen?" I watched him immediately slip it on. Twisting it around, he shook his hand, pointing his fingers downward. The ring fell to his lap. *I knew God led me to where I was so far, and I again had to place more trust in our Father. Calmed, I accepted this very logical occurrence and knew in my heart that stress and anxiety had brought me to such wariness; I needed to keep the faith.* Bill looked up at Shaye, "Thank you, baby. Val, will you keep this safe for me? I don't ever want to lose it."

His words were so reassuring, ah... I was smiling, and I put Bill's ring on the same chain that held my cross. "I'll keep it close to my heart, honey."

***

During the next five days, Bill had physical therapy, played games to strengthen his brain, and relearned tasks, like writing a check. In his spare time he watched TV. Sesame Street became his favorite show. Bill had been doing so well with all his activities; I was so proud of his extraordinary accomplishments.

On June 2nd we practiced going home. A man from physical therapy and a woman from speech therapy joined Bill and me during lunch.

"Mr. Faulkner, we would like your wife to pull her car around to the side door. We're going to see if you can walk out there and get in the vehicle. This is only a practice." The gentleman looked at his watch. "Finish your lunch. We'll figure about half hour."

"Okay."

Bill and I both thought this was pretty ridiculous but went along with the rehearsal, careful to do what we were told. It was hot outside, and I cranked the air conditioning as I waited. I could see he was having some difficulty opening the door and manipulating the walker. Cautiously persisting, he gradually made it to the Jeep and opened the door.

"Hey, great job! Keep up the good work."

"Whew, it's hot out here." Sweat was beading on his brow. Maneuvering his walker away from the car door, Bill climbed in the front seat and fastened his seat belt, all the while being watched by the directors of this show. Unzipping his window, he took a bow and gave them his last line: "I'm leaving... Val, go... now!"

Bill's panicked audience leapt foreword with frenzy - didn't they realize he was joking? Watching the scene unfold, I laughed out loud. Bill was such a character. Bill smiled at me, and looking very sure of him-self, he yelled. "GO!"

It took about twenty minutes to persuade him he had to get out of the jeep. Overall, I was relieved to hear the incident hadn't affected his ratings.

Although the last part of his therapy was torture, Bill's compliance and reasoning capabilities allowed him a certificate of completion. The medical staff at Northbay Rehabilitation Center brought us the good news on June 3rd, not even a month after Bill's aneurysm.

"Mr. Faulkner, you're better off than most people. Some have remained in rehab for six months and haven't come close to what you have accomplished. You can go home."

Chapter 25

We were on our own. Other than some outpatient appointments at rehab, I was in charge of Bill's well being. I used a little less salt, a little less fat, and tied a string around my pinky to remember the vitamins. Each day I made sure we found time to exercise. I'd drive him to the mall, and we would walk in air-conditioned comfort. Bill balked, "Only old farts walk around in the mall for exercise mooching free air-conditioning."

"Sweetheart, guess what?"

"I know, don't remind me."

Setting goals, we walked a little further each day, Bill's strength gradually improving. Strolling hand in hand was a slow race back to normal, but I kept the faith. Occasionally, glimpses of his old personality resurfaced. Something would click in his brain: a memory, a moment. One afternoon, while taking a rest at the far end of the mall, I asked him, "Do you remember?"

"Not too much. I remember you and some nurse walking me in the hospital hallway. There were old people lying in their beds when we passed their rooms. Oh yeah, workers were up on the roof. I could see them out my window, watching from my bed; really not much else."

"Do you remember the day it happened?"

"I know we went to Kathie and Dave's to do some work at their condo; it was Friday. I can't remember anything after that."

"What about Katie's jazz band concert?"

"That was last year, wasn't it?"

"No, it was the Saturday before you went to the hospital."

"You're pulling my leg! That was over a year ago...are you sure?"

"Positive. I wouldn't kid about that. We went to Katie's concert on Saturday night, and on Mother's Day we went to the Greek Church to watch Stacie's husband perform with the Richey Orchestra."

Bill, with a silly grin on his face, responded, "Sorry, Val. That's all Greek to me."

"Woo, woo...good one." I smiled back. I had to be careful not to push him too much, though. I could see a stress line above his brow. He joked, but Bill didn't like it when he couldn't solve a problem. "Okay, are we ready? Some more laps? Or should we just get going?"

"Let's get going, Val. I'm done for today."

***

I continually worked on improving our routine, letting Bill expect – rather than guess – what was next. I challenged myself to see if I could organize his everyday tasks into an orderly schedule. The doctors had mentioned more than once, *"Repeating something several times is beneficial."* Since he went to outpatient rehab on Mondays, Wednesdays, and Fridays, it seemed logical to set aside time on Tuesdays and Thursdays for his homework. Taking two weeks at a time, I planned our agenda. Using a chart, I inserted timeslots for his medications as well.

I was cleaning up after dinner while Bill worked on his assignments. I smiled as I checked him out through the kitchen window. I felt as though I deserved a medal; this schedule thing was really working. He was making such an effort; my heart beamed with pride for him. Hurrying with the dishes, I couldn't wait to go give him a great big hug.

I dried my hands and poured some coffee. Gently placing a steaming mug on the table for Bill, I looked over his shoulder. He was doing a crossword puzzle!

"Did you do your homework?" I demanded.

"No, not yet I have plenty of time."

"No, you don't. You go tomorrow."

"I know. It's on the schedule."

Two hours before Bill's appointment with the therapist, he finally sat down at the table to start the homework, *so much for my award-winning schedule.* I checked on him about twenty minutes later. He was outside doing another crossword.

"Gees, Bill. Did you finish your work?"

"Yeah, piece of cake."

"You know, if you mess up they may put you back in the slammer."

"Got it covered, honey." He didn't miss a beat, "I just need seventeen down."

***

Arriving at the rehab, the therapist had us sit down in her office.

"Do you have your assignment, Mr. Faulkner?" I watched Bill hand her his papers, feeling like we were back in school, and he'd been hauled to the office. Had he done them okay?

Bill piped up, "Sure do. I think there's a mistake in question number thirty-two. The answer should be 236. The only choice close was 235. I could be wrong…"

Reviewing the questions she said, "Nice work. Your handwriting is a little shaky. Other than that, you did very well." Grabbing her calculator, she went over question thirty-two. "Oops, our mistake; you're correct, excellent job, Mr. Faulkner."

Bill looked over at me and stuck out his tongue; I rolled my eyes and thought about smacking him but reconsidered. I laughed, "You're such a smart aleck! Good going."

The therapist continued: "Well, it looks like you're recovering nicely, any headaches?"

"No, I feel great. I get kind of tired when I take that blood pressure pill. It really wipes me out for a couple of hours. Other than that, I'm cool."

"Very well, as far as I'm concerned you're on your way to a full recovery. I don't think we'll need to see you again unless you have a problem. Congratulations, Mr. Faulkner! Very rarely do we see such great results. You have been blessed."

***

For the rest of the summer and into the fall, we strived for perfection and achieved many of our goals. Bill was astonishing, and there wasn't a day that I didn't give thanks. He was driving. He was top notch in his physical and mental skills, and we even went back to work. He was a walking, talking miracle. There was just one thing missing. Daydreams of the past were breaking my heart.

I seemed to be the only one that was aware of a difference in our enchanted life. I couldn't stop thinking about the way we used to be. Bill was totally recovered to everyone, except me. I had spent my life with this man, and I felt there was an important link missing in our relationship. I wondered if medication was the cause or if he had lost vital cells during the incident, or was it something else? Was it something I would have to wait for, to understand? It had been so long since we'd made love. Attempts made after Bill came home were hollow. We were mechanical, just going through the motions. Scared, fear had triggered emotions neither of us could tame. The trauma held us in its vicious claws. How could we let the monster win? We didn't quite know what was wrong. I knew no one was to blame. This was life, but why? I couldn't understand it. I believed God had a plan for each of us... but I wanted the man I loved. I needed his touch. How could I ask for more? I'd had so many blessings.

I confided in Joyce, and she gave me her best explanation. Bill was flat. I agreed this was a perfect synonym and wondered what could help him to feel again. His motivation levels were stationary, and he didn't have anything that could stimulate any particular lows or highs in his daily attitude. Just even, straight...flat. I couldn't condone this state although I tried, and then I told her I felt he was contagious. I was feeling the same way more often than not. Ambitions and dreams were slipping, dwindling away, far from our reach. We were existing. Just existing and time was passing, the precious time we had been given.

Shaye offered her opinion and told me I needed a hobby. I took her advice and began painting again, something I hadn't done since Stacie was a baby. I attempted to get Bill interested in something fun, but he seemed content with doing nothing during his off time. Television blared at him and he seemed mesmerized hour after hour, content to sit and stare, no need for interaction with anybody....anyone including me.

***

Six months later, Christmas was approaching, and I found even my most favorite time of year was more of an effort than a joy. I brought down all the boxes of decorations, and Bill halfheartedly helped me decorate. I did some online shopping for the grandkids and went through the motions of the season but found no spirit in any of the over commercialization taking place at this time of year. With only a few days left before Christmas, I decided to go to Dillard's and see if I could find a present for Bill. I meandered around the men's clothing searching for the perfect gift. I went through the motions and gathered a few items but knew the duty of shopping was all I was feeling. I coordinated a jacket and pants and since I wanted to finish with a shirt, I wandered around finding nothing. I stopped in front of a rack when I heard the song "I'll be home for Christmas" beginning. It wasn't long before tears were trickling down my cheeks. I swiped my eyes and cursed the emotions that I was feeling. That song had always made me cry because it made me remember a time when I was alone. This day the memory was real. I didn't want to have this lonely, isolated feeling. How could God do this?

"May I help you?"

I turned to see a tiny, little lady. She appeared of oriental heritage. Her attire was soft and flowing, not totally business like and her graying hair was pulled gently back in a soft bun. She wore a Dillard's name tag and 'Ta' was written on the line for her name. Her dark eyes slanted and she curiously waited for my answer. "Oh I'm just looking... I need a shirt to go with these." I held out my choices and she looked, then immediately began her own search. She faded into the racks and shelves, and I was surprised about fifteen minutes later when she came back holding a shirt.

"I lost you; how about this?" I checked the three pieces, and the shirt was definitely perfect.

"How much?" Ta found the tag and quoted me forty-five dollars. "Umm... That's a bit more than ..." I kept looking and thought how nice everything looked. Sighing, "What the heck....it's perfect." We walked to the cashier's desk, and she began to ring me up.

She gently placed each item out on the counter. Tissue paper was placed between the folds of the pants, and Ta smoothed out each wrinkle to assure they would look beautiful in the gift box. She did the same for the jacket. She looked up at me, "Are these all for the same person?"

"Yes, my husband."

"He is a very lucky man. You have picked such beautiful things for him."

"Well it's Christmas….I wanted to spoil him, I guess." I was thinking about the shirt and how expensive it was. I watched her as she finished so flawlessly with each piece." I guess I can spoil him a little bit more this year…. Last May I almost lost him." Ta looked up at me with questions in her eyes, so I continued. I told her about Bill and how fortunate I was to have him with me. As I explained to her she smiled sweetly as though I was telling her a story. For some reason I felt the spirit coming into my life, and I enjoyed our conversation. Then she told me I was very lucky to have my husband with me for Christmas.

"Last year about the same time, my husband had a stroke. We were married forty-three years. He called me and said he called 911, and I should meet him at the hospital. I met him at the hospital, and we talked before surgery. The doctors told me the surgery… Well, eighty percent are just fine. The doctor didn't think there would be any problems. But there were and my husband … he never came out, alive." Her eyes filled with tears, and she stopped speaking.

I went to the other side of the counter. "I'm so sorry….. Oh my God, I am so sorry." I hugged her and we wept together. Two woman feeling pain…..But I still had a chance; hers was gone. I felt my heart breaking for her.

Then she looked up at me and said," You know I had a wonderful life. You must take care of your man and have one, too. Have a wonderful Christmas; cherish him. Come back and see me sometime. I have liked talking to you." I looked into her face and could see a woman with such strength. "God Bless you both."

"Thank you, may God bless you too… Merry Christmas."

As the days and weeks passed, I thought of what Ta had said. 'Take care of your man, cherish him.' The angel at Dillard's gave me my strength. I found understanding and patience and held on to my faith.

***

May 2006: It was just about a year since Bill had had the aneurysm. I decided to retire early. "Bill, I need a quick shower. I'm going up."

Bill was watching TV. "Okay, I'll be up in a little bit."

I washed my hair and shaved my legs. The hot water streamed down my body mingling with my thoughts. I weighed out the positive; so many blessings. Life was going on, and I was realizing that time could heal many problems and gradually my fears were diminishing. I thanked God that I didn't agonize every time Bill went upstairs. Little by little, life discovered new meaning, and we held tight to each other as we climbed our mountains.

Unexpectedly, I heard the door open, then close and felt a little draft. I looked up to see two blue eyes looking at me with eyebrows wiggling up and down.

"Hello, little girl, want some company?"

I couldn't help but giggle. *Some things never change.* "Sure, big boy, you can wash my back."

"Actually, I was interested in a lot more than just your back." With that he gave my bottom a playful smack. "What a sweet backside it is."

"Watch it, mister!" He picked up the soap and a wash cloth and gently massaged my back.

"This is a surprise."

"I was watching a TV show about a man who was in a coma for seven years.

"Really..." I was enjoying the pleasant feeling brought on by his attention.

"His wife left him. The doctors told her he would never wake up, and she couldn't handle it and filed for divorce. Now he's all alone.

"Gees... Life can get so messed up."

"I'm so lucky to have you, Val. I love you and I need you. I was thinking about how wonderful it would be to hold you in my arms and feel your body next to mine. I know how long it's been, but I really need your love tonight. It's time for me to wake up and start living again." I turned around and Bill held me in his arms. We kissed under the spray, the first time in a long time. Everything felt right. I looked to Bill's eyes to see if he felt it too, the devotion we had shared....the thrill....the sparks. We played in the shower for about twenty minutes, lathering and rinsing each other. Renewing our love and immersed in the moment. The clear water washed away any doubts, and when we were finished showering, we both felt glory in this unexpected moment.

Bill left me in the shower to dry himself off. "Honey, I left you a little something. It's out here by the towels."

I recalled this cherished feeling, and a warm memorable glow embraced me. While I dried my hair, I noticed the little something, my nightie. It had been Bill's favorite. I could hear a hint of music softly playing through the door. I slipped into the teddy; short, black, and way too shear, and I combed my hair, letting it fall down the middle of my back. The mirror reflected my feelings; my heart had begun to flutter with anticipation. I opened the door to the bedroom. Standing in the doorway I gazed out at the soft glow of romance.

"Bill, it's beautiful." The room was lit by eight or nine scented candles. He was already waiting, propped on a few pillows, a bath towel wrapped around his waist.

"Val, you look just like you did on our honeymoon. Come over here, sweetheart. I need a closer look." He let out a soft whistle of approval as I edged to the side of the bed. I felt my face turning shades of pink as I became aware of the look in Bill's eyes. Oh, how I wanted him to think I was pretty; how I wanted him to want me, to need me.

Bill held out his hand as I climbed into bed. "I need to hold you close." Sliding his arm around my waist, he pulled me gently towards him. Feeling the heat of his skin next to mine, we lay pressing our bodies together. Bill touched me tenderly; his hand moved gently over me and rested at the small of my back. I kissed his neck and chin and nibbled at his lips. Ever so sweetly, he traced my curves with an undeniable longing. In the dim light our affectionate kisses rekindled the flames of our passion. That night we began again; we discovered each other and brought love back into our lives. There was harmony, a love song playing that only we could hear. Rhythm kept time by the strum of our hearts, a breathtaking crescendo to the very last beat.

Later, while we cuddled in each other's arms, basking in such sweet bliss, we didn't say a word. We knew God had brought us together... through sickness and health, till death do us part.

Bill blew out the last candle. "I love you, Val."

"I love you more..."

Epilogue

*"**D**id I not tell you and promise you that if you would believe and rely on me, you would see the glory of God?"*

John 11:40

I found this verse just weeks before completing the book. I can't say I was surprised. There were a number of times that God undeniably lead me in the right direction. Once the power blinked and the computer shut down, I hadn't had the chance to hit save. I assumed He didn't feel that chapter was necessary. Another time I was writing and attempting to be funny. I looked up from the computer to see the word 'Lies'. I gasped, and you can be sure I haven't even stretched the truth about any or all circumstances involving the stories. I laugh with Bill when I recall the time I was on a roll. I had four fingers typing away, and I watched in amazement at my speed and ability on the computer keyboard. When I glanced up to the screen, yes...you guessed. It was blank. So...I am ecstatic to have accomplished my task, but in all honesty I have to thank our Lord once again. I couldn't have done this on my own.

Each and every day I depend on God to assist me. I walk this life, and I see the wonders God has given me and the love that He has shown. I am amazed to find Him everywhere. In a child's face, a lonely man's hand, ordinary people with an extraordinary kindness....an ability to love. I Praise you Father for giving me the words, the stories, and most of all allowing me to feel your spirit.

Spending that day at the fireplace hearth, I only imagined what it would be like to finish my writing. I'd made a promise; I've kept my word. Thank you Jesus; because of You, it's all come together, Lord. I thank you for your blessings. I believe in this chapter of my life; You carried me through, beginning to end. You have been with me at the highest peaks as well as the lowest valleys. *I trusted and believed.*

I've learned don't worry about the future. Today, I'll go back to doing electrical work with my husband. Side by side, we'll work; we'll laugh. We'll encourage; we'll give praise. *I will rely on You.*

I've learned to appreciate every second. At the end of the day when the evening comes, we'll cherish our moments together. Thank you, Lord for love. *I have seen the glory of God.*

I've learned that You live in so many hearts...thank you, Lord, for being in mine. I promise that each time I squeeze Bill's hand three times, and every time I hear a siren scream....... I will never forget your blessings; I know Bill will never forget.......

Because of You, and Your amazing grace, we'll be able tell the stories together.

About the Author

Valerie was raised on Long Island, about two hours east of New York City. In the fifties and sixties her hometown Yaphank, was rural, woods and fields housed just a handful of dwellings. Growing up in a small town did not mean that Valerie would not have big dreams.

In 1973 she and her husband and their first child began a new adventure as they left family and friends and moved to Florida. As their family grew by two more children Valerie had the luxury of being a stay-at-home mom during the primary years of their lives. This did not hinder another adventure however as she and her husband began an electrical contracting business in 1973. Valerie managed home, children and office while Bill worked out in the field. As the children became more independent Valerie dabbled in other endeavors including waiting tables and baby sitting as she brought in a little extra family income. Meanwhile husband Bill continued to cultivate Faulkner Electric, Inc. Which has now been a successful business for over thirty-five years.

At one time the couple had many employees and tackled large construction projects but over the past eight years they have downsized to a team of two. As Valerie became adept in the hands on part of the electrical business in addition to skills she had in office management, she began working as an electrician with Bill on a daily basis.

They continue to reside on the west coast of Florida

in a town called Port Richey. Their three grown children and their families live nearby as well as Valerie's sisters and parents. When the clan gets together they make up about forty in all, last count.

Valerie is a woman of faith and enjoys life and all her blessings. She is not wealthy but is certainly rich. She is a typical American that never gives up. She believes in the promise of tomorrow.

During the course of writing her first novel Valerie's daughter gave her a compliment that she holds in high regard. Her daughter said, "Mom, I know I know you, but while reading your book I realized you are a very special person with an extraordinary story to tell." Simply put she finished with, "If I didn't know you already, you'd be a person I'd definitely like to meet."

www.ingramcontent.com/pod-product-compliance
Lightning Source LLC
LaVergne TN
LVHW051627080426
835511LV00016B/2215